PENGUIN BOOKS

LITERARY AGENTS

Debby Mayer has published fiction, essays, and journalism. After working for Poets & Writers for several years, she now writes and edits for an independent newspaper in upstate New York.

For information about Poets & Writers, Inc., please see page 171.

Literary Agents

THE ESSENTIAL GUIDE FOR WRITERS

Debby Mayer

PENGUIN BOOKS

PENGUIN BOOKS
Published by the Penguin Group
Penguin Putnam Inc., 375 Hudson Street,
New York, New York 10014, U.S.A.
Penguin Books Ltd, 27 Wrights Lane,
London W8 5TZ, England
Penguin Books Australia Ltd, Ringwood,
Victoria, Australia
Penguin Books Canada Ltd, 10 Alcorn Avenue,
Toronto, Ontario, Canada M4V 3B2
Penguin Books (N.Z.) Ltd, 182–190 Wairau Road,
Auckland 10, New Zealand

Penguin Books Ltd, Registered Offices:
Harmondsworth, Middlesex, England

Literary Agents by Judith Johnson Sherwin first published
in the United States of America by Poets & Writers, Inc. 1978
Revised edition by Debby Mayer published 1983
Second revised edition by Debby Mayer published 1988
Third revised edition by Adam Begley published in Penguin Books 1993
This fourth revised edition by Debby Mayer published 1998

1 3 5 7 9 10 8 6 4 2

LIBRARY OF CONGRESS CATALOGING IN PUBLICATION DATA
Mayer, Debby.
Literary agents: the essential guide for writers/Debby Mayer.
p. cm.
"Poets & Writers is pleased to present the revised fifth edition"—
Introd.
Rev. ed. of: Literary agents. 3rd rev. ed./Adam Begley, 1993.
ISBN 0 14 02.6873 1 (pbk.)
1. Literary agents.   I. Begley, Adam.   Literary agents.
II. Poets & Writers, Inc.   III. Title.
PN163.M386   1998
070.5'2—dc21   97–34446

Printed in the United States of America
Set in Fairfield Light
Designed by Alice Sorensen

FOREWORD

We all know that everything was better before we came
on the scene (or so we are always told): Paris was more
beautiful, Florence entertained only a trickle of tourists,
whooping cranes lived on the river. And everything was
cheaper.

It was also, in the old days, easier to find an agent.
But what are we to do about it? Fortunately, the business
of finding an agent, while more difficult than it used to
be, and more costly, is not yet impossible. It takes pa-
tience, resourcefulness, and care, but they're still out
there and agents, like publishers, need writers as much
as we need them.

There are two reasons the getting has gotten tougher
lately. Canny, sophisticated writers have so proliferated in
the last couple of decades, many of them trained in writ-

ing programs to know what they need, that there is a lot more competition for representation than there has ever been.

And secondly, as the publishing world changes and the market shrinks for certain kinds of books (notably "literary" fiction, the kind that satisfies many of us but leaves the keepers of the corporate bottom line shaking their heads), many agents are more wary than ever before of taking on books with "noncommercial" scrawled in invisible ink across their manuscript boxes. And yet, a walk through a good bookstore tells us that such books *are* being published. Even first novels are there to be bought and read. The editors of small and university presses are pleased these days that books, which once were comfortably housed at trade publishers, are finding their way onto their desks now, their authors happy to be taken on for very little money, scant promotional budgets and uncertain distribution but—in compensation—frequently more respectful editing and far greater attention from the rest of the staff. Agents are sending them books now, perhaps not exactly happily (because that's no way to make a killing) but gratefully nonetheless.

The news is far better for the writers of non-fiction, for whom, in this news-hungry time, there are still avid readers and a proliferation of spin-off and marketing possibilities. I heard recently about a contract that included a "beach fly-over," presumably by a crop-duster waving the book's title on a flapping pennant. (I'm planning to insist on sky-writing in my next contract.)

I "got" my agent, and she "got" me, a long time ago

when the getting was, I admit, easier—eight books ago, to be exact, most of which brought her enough profit to buy herself a bouquet of roses to celebrate her kindness and her belief in my "potential," but not much more. A poet-turned-short story writer who had never dreamed of acquiring an agent, I was advised by the editor to whom I had innocently taken my first book of fiction that I needed a protector. "Someone," she said forthrightly, "who works for *you*, not for the publisher, no matter how nice I might *seem*." Provoked by visions of foxes in the hen-house and Red Riding Hood flattered by the wolf, I used the short list she provided and was redirected by some-body who was "full up"—a very common problem—to a friend of hers who was just starting her own agency. (Though novices may only be learning the ropes, still there is no better time to find an agent than just after they've opened their doors for business.)

The friend was modest enough to think she ought to introduce herself to me by laying out her background and her philosophy, and not simply assume I'd take her on blindly and gratefully. This was either a sign of her un-derstanding that without a track record she had to woo me, or the outcome of a less desperate buyer's market, or of her innate decency and sensitivity. (All three, I suspect.)

She has, I like to say, stuck with me through much thin and a little thick. Twenty-five years later, because she takes such good care of my work and my psyche, I am still with Virginia Barber; I think I am her client of longest standing. I have dedicated a book to her; so has

Alice Munro. (Such dedications should be duly noted by aspiring writers and followed-up on. They are the gold medals in a business that proceeds on more intangible matters than financial indebtedness.)

The hard fact is that because many writers in search of an agent find themselves in a seller's market, when someone shows an interest in their work they are too abject with gratitude to exercise the kind of care they'd routinely expend on other, less significant, choices in their lives. Bearing in mind that many feel so beggared by the process that they don't dare to be choosy, still I asked both my agent and my editor what single caveat they would have for a writer going out on the market.

My agent, Virginia Barber, said without hesitation—please note, these are not exact quotes; I am a fiction writer—Be sure *that* agent feels he or she can sell *that* book. Has a plan for it, understands its particular needs, doesn't intend to shop it around arbitrarily.

My editor, John Glusman of Farrar, Straus & Giroux, added, with equal firmness, be wary of agents who promise the world. There are a lot of agents of dubious integrity who are resented by publishers because they act like sharks. In the short run, he said, they seem to serve a writer well, but in the end editors shudder when they see them coming, and that's counter-productive. Agents have enduring and complex relationships with publishing houses, and people have long memories.

Both cautions echo my own most fundamental suggestion: you have to know what you need in an agent—a friend or a more impersonal business associate; a critic who will participate (to a point, which you must set) in thinking about and revising your work, or someone who would not dream of intruding on the work itself.

You have the right to make inquiries into your potential agent's personal style and modus operandi, and you shouldn't (even if you're feeling desperate) hire someone whom you are not comfortable with, or who seems prepared to show your book in a manner that violates your standards. Such liaisons may seem preferable in the short run to get your book published; but your agent is your representative to the publishing world, and therefore represents *you*. Since anyone can set up shop to be an agent—there is neither degree nor licensure nor any requisite beyond will and wit, plus office space, telephone, and letterhead—you as writer need to maintain the dignity of your expectations and your understanding of your work. Otherwise you are merely postponing the inevitable day of professional divorce, and that is always awkward and painful.

As my own agent said during our last contract negotiation, as she was laying out her strategy, "And if your publishers reject this, remember, I'm the one who'll take the flak. That's what I'm here for." When I passed on to her the compliment that my editor had told me what a pleasure it was to work with her, she laughed and said "That must mean I didn't ask for enough!" But she was pleased and so was I. I may have my art; she certainly has hers.

Rosellen Brown

CONTENTS

INTRODUCTION

Poets & Writers is pleased to present the revised fifth edition of *Literary Agents: The Essential Guide for Writers*, by Debby Mayer, published by Penguin Books.

Since 1970 Poets & Writers has been the central source of practical information for writers in the United States. Writers are solitary workers, and the services of Poets & Writers help fill their need for community, communication, and professional information.

The staff of Poets & Writers meet writers at conferences and seminars throughout the country. And the organization answers thousands of questions each year on such subjects as copyright, query letters, and agents. Questions about how to work with a literary agent run second only to queries about how to get published and the two often intersect.

The first chapter of this book answers the two questions writers most often have about agents:

- What exactly does a literary agent do?

- How much does an agent charge?

How to find an agent and the terms of the writer-agent agreement are covered in chapters two and three. In chapter four, established agents and authors talk about the business. This is followed by a list of agents who will consider unsolicited material without charging a reading fee.

Poets & Writers offers this book as a guide to writers who, in addition to working at their craft, must take responsibility for the often frustrating job of guiding their manuscript to publication. We hope this book will ease the journey for writers working with agents to accomplish that task.

The list of agents at the back of this book was expertly researched and compiled by Lynn McCary. We thank Lynn for her stellar work. We are also grateful to Joseph Regal at Russell & Volkening for his comments on the rights chart appearing on page 45, and to Caroline White at Penguin Books for her graciousness and guidance.

Elliot Figman
Executive Director
Poets & Writers, Inc.

Literary Agents

CHAPTER ONE

The Literary Agent: Who Needs One and Why?

I F a book appears in bookstores bearing the imprint of a major publisher, the chances are excellent that the author is represented by a literary agent. Any writer with a publishable manuscript or a viable proposal will try to hire the services of an agent. Most well-known and commercially successful authors who can pick and choose among competing publishers use an agent as a buffer to distance themselves from the messy details of negotiations and contracts and royalty statements. The agent takes care of the business; the writer sticks to writing.

Some authors come to rely on their agents for literary advice, others for stability. In theory, a writer need only go through the process of finding an agent once, whereas each new book usually requires a new contract, sometimes a new editor, or even a new publisher. Editors change houses, often without warning; publishing companies go out of business, merge with other houses, or redefine themselves entirely. Faced with these uncertainties, most writers look to an agent for continuity.

Some writers fall into a relationship with a particular publishing house and never feel the need for an intermediary; others make a conscious choice to deal directly with their publishers. But as publishing and subsidiary rights contracts became more complicated in the 1990s, even those writers traditionally known for not having literary agents went over to the other side. Stephen King is now represented by Chuck Verrill of Darhansoff & Verrill. Stephen Dixon, who published 14 novels and 500 short stories without an agent, asked Kim Witherspoon of Witherspoon Associates to represent his fiction after he felt a publisher treated him unfairly (see Chapter Four).

In some extreme cases—brand-name authors and starving poets, for example—agents can be less than useful or prohibitively expensive.

For a writer who can confidently expect generous offers from many publishers for each book, a lawyer with publishing expertise who bills at an hourly rate might make more sense than an agent who charges a 15-percent commission. Lawyer-agents market a manuscript, haggle with an editor over contractual clauses, and settle any disputes that may arise during the publishing process. The drawback to a writer represented by a lawyer is that the writer will have to monitor royalty statements, keep records, and handle business correspondence, tasks that would otherwise fall to an agent. Their bills reflect time spent on the job, not the kind of work done. An agent who works on a commission basis, on the other hand, earns money only when the writer does.

Lawyer-agents point out that they save their clients money: the bigger the deal, the bigger the savings. Most literary agents would earn about $300,000 on a $2 million contract; a lawyer charging $375 per hour would earn closer to $30,000.

For an author negotiating an advance of $75,000 or even $150,000, $375 per hour begins to seem relatively expensive, however, and marketing a book and negotiating a contract require a certain amount of time, regardless of the money involved.

At the other end of the earnings scale, only rarely will an agent agree to represent a writer who does not make money and is not ever likely to. This excludes most poets and many short story writers from literary agent circles. Relatively little negotiation is involved in selling a poem or short story to a literary magazine or small press, and the income from such sales, while precious to the writer, is rarely enough to interest an agent. (Of 290 agents surveyed for this book, only 4 said they would consider taking on a prospective client who sent in a collection of poems.)

Hopeful first-time authors often send their work directly to publishing houses for the simple reason that they can't convince an agent to represent them—it can be nearly as difficult for an unknown writer to find an agent as to find an editor at an appropriate publishing house. And yet many publishers neglect, ignore, or flatly reject manuscripts that are not submitted by agents. This is the widely recognized and much lamented double bind that welcomes the newcomer to the curious world of book publishing.

In the end, "standard practice" seems most sensible: a writer who has in hand a marketable property—that is, a book-length work or a proposal for a book-length work —should consider hiring an agent. This advice is offered to first-time authors and battle-scarred veterans alike; it covers books already in print as well as manuscripts fresh from the typewriter (a writer can decide that he or she needs to be represented by an agent at any point in the publishing process). But advice should always come weighted with a caveat, and in this case there are two: a bad agent can be worse than no agent, and all agents, even the most effective, are at best a necessary evil. In the best of all possible worlds, writers and publishers would work in concert, with no need for a middleman. But nearly all publishing companies are concerned first and foremost with their own profit margins. Authors generally have other things in mind, whether they are marketing possibilities or literary excellence. Agents try to bridge the gap between the author's hopes and the reality offered by the publisher.

WHAT DOES A LITERARY AGENT DO?

A good agent promotes and protects the writer's interests by finding a suitable editor at a suitable publishing house, negotiating a favorable contract, watching over the publishing process, collecting all payments due, and keeping accurate records. The best agents also plan for the future; they advise their authors on how to manage a successful career. Thus an effective agent becomes the author's sales representative, business manager, and consultant.

Sometimes this relationship grows into close friendship. But at the outset, writer and agent meet on professional ground. Here are some of the things an agent can do for a writer.

The Hunt for an Editor

Few writers are familiar with more than a handful of editors; most know the names of a half dozen prominent publishing houses, and that's it. The agent, however, is presumed to be reasonably well acquainted not only with a wide range of publishers, from tiny independent presses to multinational conglomerates, but also with the key editors at each establishment. The agent can put this knowledge to use in the following ways:

- Formulating a sales pitch. The agent should have a general plan for how to sell the writer's work and also know how to tailor the presentation to fit the taste of individual editors.

- Submitting only to appropriate houses. This means avoiding unstable publishing companies as well as those with a history of poor performance with the kind of book on offer.

- Making sure the project receives due con-
  sideration. An agent with a good reputation
  should have some clout and extensive personal
  contacts.

- Matching the writer with the right editor. Just
  because an editor shows interest in a particular
  project doesn't mean the editor and the writer
  will work well together.

- Sending out multiple submissions. When a proposal or manuscript is mailed to several publishers at once, the whole process moves faster
  (agents do this routinely, but publishers sometimes disapprove of writers who try it themselves).

- Finding foreign publishers, usually with the
  help of foreign-based subagents (see page 43).

Getting to Yes

For some writers, an agent's most important function
is negotiating the contract, and the important part of
the negotiation is the dollar amount of the advance.
Anyone who has struggled to earn a living as a writer
will understand this itch to quickly earn large sums
of money. But a good agent is thinking about much
more than the size of the first payment.

To the layman, the contracts issued by publishing
houses are complicated documents even in their ba-

sic "boilerplate" form. Agents usually seek to make changes in these contracts or add clauses beneficial to the writer. When the legal and financial intricacies have all been hammered out, the agent should be able to present the writer with an agreement suited to his or her needs. An agent may try to arrange the best possible deal by doing any of the following:

- Conducting an auction to obtain a larger advance or more favorable terms. Auctions are appropriate only to projects with broad appeal and good commercial prospects; moreover, the book must be suited to a number of different houses.

- Retaining certain subsidiary rights. Publishers want to buy as many rights as possible, and in some cases the writer does well to sell them. The publisher, however, is not always in the business of making money for the writer, so a writer's interests may be better served if the agent can manage to curb the publisher's acquisitive instinct and keep some rights for the writer (see "Rights for Sale," page 43).

- Arranging a schedule of payments that meets the author's immediate and long-term needs. Some well-paid writers prefer to receive their advance in regular installments rather than wait for lump sums on uncertain dates fixed by convention, such as on delivery of the completed manuscript or on the publication date.

- Requesting contract clauses that stipulate certain conditions. For example, a minimum advertising and promotion budget, a minimum first printing, or authorial control over jacket design (publishers don't often accept these kinds of conditions, but on the other hand agents don't often insist).

- Adding bonus clauses tied to the book's performance, including number of copies shipped, appearance(s) on the best-seller list, the release of a movie, or appearance of a television version.

The Follow-Through

The popular image of the agent wheeling and dealing, always in the thick of the action, is the product of a basic misconception. The spotlight is on when an agent strikes a lucrative deal: the media descend, report on the stunning coup, and vanish. But most of the work, much of it dull routine, goes on before and, especially, after the contract has been negotiated, and many good, solid deals don't make headlines. As long as the book is in print, and as long as there is any interest (or the prospect of any interest) in the rights attached to it, the agent should be on the job. In the months and years after a contract is signed, the agent's less glamorous duties include

- Resolving any conflicts between author and editor or author and publisher.

- Monitoring the publishing process to ensure that the terms of the contract are fulfilled.

- Obtaining prompt royalty statements, verifying their accuracy, and, if possible, explaining them to the author (there are few documents more impenetrable to the uninitiated than a publisher's royalty statement).

- Collecting all payments due the author. The money a book earns under contracts negotiated by the agent is generally sent directly to the agent, who then deducts the agency commission, plus expenses, before passing payment on to the author (this arrangement persists as long as the contracts are in force, even if author and agent part company).

- Selling any rights not already sold to the publisher.

- Recording printing histories and sales records.

- Handling mail sent to the author care of the agent.

Taking the Long View

Of the many ways in which an agent can foster a writer's career, giving sound advice can be the most important. Not all agents are equally well equipped for dispensing wisdom, and yet almost every agent knows enough to weigh today's choices against tomorrow's prospects. It's especially important that young writers develop a sense of how to build an audience, how to forge a lasting connection with a publisher, and how to respond to media attention. Even established authors can benefit from a shrewd analysis of the current publishing climate.

There's no standard prescription for what kind of counsel an agent should provide, and this is certainly not the kind of service that can be outlined in any formal agreement between an author and his or her agent. However, an agent may help to shape a writer's future by

- Suggesting changes to a proposal or a manuscript. Publishers are less and less likely these days to accept material that they feel will require substantial revision, and so agents sometimes act as editors to make sure that submitted work has found its finished form.

- Introducing a writer who is "between books" to an editor who has a project in mind (the books that result from this kind of matchmaking are almost always nonfiction).

- Offering to submit the writer's work to low- or non-paying prestige publications.

- Discouraging ill-conceived projects.

WHAT IF A WRITER *NEEDS* EDITORIAL HELP?

Agents and editors have very different jobs. While many agents say that more and more they are assuming an editorial role (they claim to shape their clients' proposals and polish their manuscripts), the essential distinction has not changed: an agent represents an author's work; an editor edits it for publication. If an agent markets a manuscript, a commission should be the reward for success. If an agent reads and evaluates a manuscript, the professional titles have been misappropriated—the agent is in fact an editor.

A writer who needs help with a manuscript can always hire an accredited professional. There is a section devoted to Editorial Services in the 1997 *Literary Market Place*. Writers can also consult *Poets & Writers Magazine* which, along with other trade publications, includes listings from editors and writers offering manuscript critique.

Writing workshops, seminars, and conferences— more than two hundred listed in the 1997 *Writers Conferences List* published by Poets & Writers—are offered year-round all over the country. Many of the conferences attract publishers, editors, and literary agents, all of whom are there in part to scout new talent. The help available to a writer at workshops and conferences may not be as precise or as practically useful as the recommendations of a freelance editor, but the experience can be both enjoyable and fruitful.

HOW MUCH DO AGENTS CHARGE?

Almost all literary agents work on a commission basis, taking either 10 or 15 percent of an author's domestic earnings. In the last ten years, the lower rate has become increasingly rare.

To gather information for this book, Poets & Writers surveyed the 290 member agents of the Association of Authors' Representatives, Inc. The Association of Authors' Representatives is a professional association of literary agents whose members do not charge writers reading fees and who agree to an eight-point canon of ethics. Of the 216 agents who responded, 120 agreed to be listed. Of those, 97 charge a 15 percent commission and 13 charge 10 percent; the remainder indicated a range, a sliding scale, or some variation. Agents may continue to offer long-time clients their lower rate and charge newcomers more, or may fix their commission according to the writer's publishing history (a first-time author will have to pay the higher rate).

It's difficult to tell a writer to disregard the commission rate when choosing an agent—after all, there's a 50-percent difference between the low and high ends of the scale. But experience suggests that the rate of commission almost never determines the success of an author-agent relationship. There are agents who ask for a 15-percent commission and then go out and double the writer's income; on the other hand, there are 10-percent agents who do very little to earn their keep.

As mentioned earlier, payments due the author are almost always sent directly to the agent, who deducts his or her commission before passing the money on.

When selling foreign rights, the agent usually works with subagents based abroad. Subagents perform in other countries most of the same tasks that the principal agent performs at home: they look for the right editor at the right house, negotiate a contract, monitor the publishing process, and collect the advance, the royalties, and any other payments due. The subagent deducts a commission (almost always 10 percent) and sends the balance to the principal agent, who also takes a cut. The two commissions on foreign sales usually add up to 20 percent.

Many agencies also deduct certain expenses from the writer's earnings. These may include

- photocopying costs

- registration and insurance of mail

- telegrams, faxes, and long-distance telephone calls

- messenger service (the publishing industry makes extensive use of New York's bicycle messengers, and somebody has to pay for them)

Note these expenses are deducted only from a writer's earnings. They should not be charged outright.

Because agencies make their money from commissions, they can seldom afford to represent writers whose work they think can't be sold. If an author earns on the average less than five thousand dollars a year from writing, the commissions won't be sufficient to interest most agents. There are, however, exceptions to this rule. Young writers in particular can find agents willing to bet on their future, at least for a book or two, and some agents continue to represent authors whose work they believe in, though it has no commercial appeal. They generally will not take on a new writer, however, if his or her book looks immediately destined for a small press or a university press. Though agents know as well as writers that a book's literary merit may have little to do with its popular success, they also know that the "small novel," the "quiet novel," the "midlist novel" that neither started nor finished a publisher's catalogue is a very hard sell these days.

And if years go by and an agent spends valuable time pitching manuscripts that are repeatedly rejected or sell for tiny sums, the writer, sad to say, will eventually be rejected, too.

CHAPTER TWO

How Does a Writer Find an Agent?

A list of the names and addresses of 120 literary agents who are members of the Association of Authors' Representatives and who do not charge reading fees begins on page 79 of this book. Staring at the agents' names, however, won't help a hopeful author pick the right one.

Establishing certain broad parameters can help the bewildered writer make a better choice. Some may decide, for instance, to consider only large, New York-based agencies; writers who live far from New York may want an agent closer to home; and some may ignore geography entirely and seek out personalized attention from a tiny agency located almost anywhere, even on another continent. This kind of decision is somewhat arbitrary: a small, well-run agency can provide better, and as varied service, as a large, poorly run agency; and though New York agencies will always claim to have the ear of the publishing industry, the fax machine has made agenting from any corner of the world perfectly feasible.

The easy way to choose is to ask for a recommendation from a friendly fellow writer, teacher, or editor. But the recommendation must cut both ways: the writer is looking for an agent worth hiring, and the agent wants to know that the writer's work is worth reading. If both conditions are met, and agent and author get along at once, the search is over. Sadly, the process is rarely that simple. Prominent agents are overwhelmed by solicitations from eager writers; their attention is hard to catch, their skepticism hard to conquer.

FINDING A WILLING AGENT

For the unknown writer, any personal recommendation helps. The best source is a book editor who has expressed serious interest in the writer's work, in part because that editor's interest will be taken as a sign of the material's commercial viability. Many editors try to maintain a purely literary relationship with their authors; they like to keep their editing tasks separate from the business aspects of acquiring a manuscript, and they prefer to negotiate a contract with the author's agent. Editors who are already interested in a writer's work are therefore often happy to furnish a short list of suitable agents.

Writing teachers are likely to know of a number of

different agents. A distinguished teacher's recommendation carries weight but isn't guaranteed to convince a busy agent. Magazine editors may also be willing to help.

Established agents say that most of their new clients are referred to them by other writers they've represented. The enthusiastic recommendation of a fellow writer is indeed an excellent calling card. Writers are often familiar only with their own agents, however, and in many cases only a writer's own agent will be swayed by a recommendation.

A writer without contacts, who has no opportunity to ask for a recommendation (or who has asked without success), will have to choose prospective agents more or less at random, approach them "cold"—that is, without prior introduction—and convince them to take on a new client.

In the acknowledgments at the beginning of many books—even novels—the author thanks his or her agent. By leafing through the hardcovers at a local bookstore, writers can easily compile a list of agents who represent works at least roughly similar to their own (and these are agents with apparently grateful clients). The next step is to get a foot in the door.

Unsolicited manuscripts, no matter how persuasive the cover letter, are automatically rejected by most agencies (and by many publishers). The writer must rely instead on the artful query—a hybrid communication that's part cover letter, part proposal, part self-promotion.

A few agents will consider a query only if it is accompanied by a credible recommendation. But of the 120 agents who agreed to be listed in this book, 118 said they would read queries sent cold through the mail. Twenty-five said they would accept telephone queries, and six said they would even read unsolicited manuscripts. A query that arrives without a self-addressed, stamped envelope for reply will almost always be ignored. Most agents discourage phone queries and the faxing of queries as well.

There are as many ways to write a query as there are to write a love letter, but one feature is essential: a concise, evocative description of the work to be marketed. An outline is helpful, and a *short* sample. Biographical information is also important. Publications should be listed in full, including small magazines, newsletters, or alternative newspapers.

There's no reason not to send out several queries at once, as long as the agents are informed. If there's been no reply to a query after three weeks, it's time to telephone and ask, politely, for a response. (Agents say they pay attention to the manners of the writers who contact them; they avoid the discourteous on the grounds that those individuals will likely be difficult to work with.)

If more than one agent expresses interest and asks to see another sample or an entire manuscript, the fortunate writer is nonetheless in a bind: many agents will only read "on exclusive." That is, they don't want to spend time on work that's also being looked at by their competitors. Yet showing the material to one agent at a time can take months.

Poets & Writers suggests the following compromise, which essentially gives the agents a limited exclusivity.

The first-choice agent gets the manuscript and is asked to give an initial response (not a firm commitment) within ten working days. If the ten days go by and no answer has been given, the second-choice agent (who has also seen a sample and responded to a query) receives a copy of the manuscript with the same request for an initial response within ten days.

This system requires tact on the part of the writer (it's not a good idea to let an agent know he or she is anything but first choice); it's also fair and relatively efficient. Some agents will not go along with it, but most will.

If no agent expresses interest after a first round of queries, subsequent rounds are certainly in order. Persistence pays in this kind of endeavor. The Association of Authors Representatives has 290 agents as members, and each of them has a different idea of what is marketable.

If, after looking for some time, a writer finds only one willing agent, the temptation to give up and take what's offered should be resisted. Most agents will accept without quibble the idea that a writer needs some time before making a firm commitment—two weeks, say. That time can be profitably spent following up on queries still pending and even contacting a few new agents. With a solid offer in hand, the writer will find this last quick round of queries surprisingly painless.

A writer suffering any real qualms about signing with a particular agent should express his or her doubts in a forthright manner and suggest that looking around for a while longer might dispel those doubts. An agent who reacts violently to the news that a prospective client is having second thoughts may very well be in the wrong business.

The writer who chooses his or her agent generally approaches the relationship with a constructive and co-operative attitude. The writer who feels stuck with the only agent who would bite makes for a less willing partner. Agents know this. Writers should be tactful and considerate about shopping around, but they should also keep in mind that in the end the agent will be happy to have been chosen.

CHOOSING AMONG WILLING AGENTS

A herd instinct motivates much of what happens in the publishing industry, and so an author with a particularly appealing manuscript or proposal may find many agents to choose from. More and more frequently in recent years, authors who receive this kind of flattering attention have been conducting formal interviews with a short list of prospective agents.

An agent who's been in business for a number of years builds a list of clients and develops a reputation among authors and editors. Listening to word of mouth, therefore, is one dependable approach to the problem of choosing an agent. But for any writer, and especially those who mistrust the industry buzz or are too far removed from publishing circles to hear it at all, there's really no substitute for direct contact of some sort with the interested agents—a long telephone call or an exchange of letters at the very least.

There are agents who will provide a complete list of their clients only to acquisitions editors in publishing houses, but even the most discreet agents will tell a prospective client what kind of writers they represent and offer to name a few by way of example. If the names provided by the agent are obscure, the writer may want to do some research. Are these reputable authors? Are the books well published? Armed with some ideas about the clients on the agent's list and a first-hand glimpse of the agent's personal style, the writer is left to make a sensitive decision that will always be based at least in part on instinct.

"I'LL TAKE BOTH"

Every now and then a clever writer decides that two agents are better than one and schemes to hire one agent for one set of rights and another for the rest. Very few agents will accept this kind of piecemeal arrangement. An agent who agrees to represent an author usually expects to take on whatever that author writes, not just one manuscript, and to handle all the associated rights for each book. Screenwriting is an exception to this rule: writers who moonlight for the movies almost always seek out a Hollywood agent in addition to their literary agent.

For most writers, one agent is plenty.

CHAPTER THREE

The Author-Agent Relationship

Mutual trust and confidence keep writer and agent working together happily. The writer trusts the agent to act with the client's best interests in mind, to give sound advice and timely support. All of a writer's earnings pass through the agent's hands, an arrangement that can survive only where confidence is certain. The agent is the writer's representative and this means that the writer must have faith that the agent won't behave in a manner grossly inconsistent with the writer's personal ethics. The agent, meanwhile, trusts the writer to continue to produce work of the quality that brought them together in the first place, and to behave in a professional manner (abiding by contracts and not withholding or falsifying information, for example). The agent expresses, through word and deed, confidence in the writer's career, a faith that may at times have to be self-sustaining. A friendly partnership should be the immediate goal of both writer and agent—fame and fortune can tag along in time.

There are, however, built-in imbalances in almost all author-agent relationships. The writer is directly responsible for what he or she writes. Any libel suits, vicious reviews, hate mail, and ridicule that come in will be directed at the writer, not at the agent. The agent negotiates the contracts, but the author signs them and is legally bound by their clauses—the agent is not. In the end, the writer claims responsibility for the direction of his or her career, regardless of how active the agent has been as an advisor and manager; triumph and failure alike can drive even well-matched partners apart. The writer has more at stake in the partnership and is far more likely to become dependent on the relationship. Last but not least, it is the writer who pays the agent. These imbalances can remain irrelevant if both parties exercise tact and restraint—but other problems can arise.

An agent is a middleman, and must foster close ties with publishers and editors at as many houses as possible. Loyalty to the client is a first principle with every good agent, and instances of outright disloyalty are extremely rare; but when an agent is negotiating with an editor and their professional ties are close and of long standing, the edge that characterizes aggressive bargaining may sometimes be missing. No matter what the connection between agent and editor, the agent knows the perils of too often seeming intransigent, or of appearing out of touch with market realities. Writers who feel that their agents could have struck a better deal can sometimes be heard muttering about the cozy arrangements between agents and publishers—they quote fondly from Shakespeare:

> Let every eye negotiate for itself
> And trust no agent.

Or as one skeptical modern-day writer put it, "When agents and editors aren't 'doing' lunch together, they're doing deals. Agents don't like the idea of jeopardizing their free lunches—the editors *always* pay—any more than they like jeopardizing their deals."

Indeed, the agent has more than one client and will soon be back at the bargaining table representing another writer's work. When the writer and the agent first come together, the agent's attention is focused on the needs of this newest client. A few months later, when the writer discovers that the agent is often too busy with some other client to come to the phone, a certain sense of disappointment is not unusual. Signed up by a top agent from a large, powerful agency, a writer sometimes finds that he or she is eventually relegated to a younger agent relatively new to the business. If the younger agent has indeed more time and energy to devote to the writer, this may be a blessing in disguise. A first-time author who landed a prominent New York agent confessed that he was very relieved to find that most of his dealings were with the agent's assistant, herself a budding agent. "She has a few clients all her own, and though I'm not really her client, she's very helpful, always available, and not at all intimidating. But when my manuscript goes out, the cover letter is signed by *my* agent"—in other words, he can still count on a prominent agent's clout.

A good agent tries to make each client feel that he or she has the agent's undivided attention. When this illusion wears thin, as it must, the writer should remember that the agent needs to work with many clients in order to earn a living; each of those clients deserves a share of the agent's time and concern.

Agents who don't provide satisfactory service, or are unable to maintain friendly and professional relationships with their clients, quickly acquire bad reputations (as do writers who are too demanding, too temperamental). When the partnership works well, when writer and agent both do their jobs, good fellowship and good income should be the result. When either party fails, both suffer.

20 QUESTIONS

The Association of Authors' Representatives, the professional association of literary agents, suggests writers ask a prospective agent the following questions

1. Is the agency a sole proprietorship? A partnership? A corporation?

2. Does the agent belong to AAR?

3. How long has the agent been in business?

4. How many people work at the agency? Of those, how many are agents? How many support staff?

5. Do specialists at the agency handle movie and television rights? Foreign rights? Are sub-agents or corresponding agents overseas and in Hollywood?

6. Does the agent represent other authors in the writer's area of interest?

7. Who in the agency will actually be handling the writer's work? Will other staff be familiar with the work and the status of the writer's business at the agency? Will the agent oversee or at least keep the writer apprised of the work the agency is doing on his/her behalf?

8. Does the agency use a contract? May the writer review a sample copy? And may the writer review the language of the agency clause that appears in contracts the agent negotiates for clients?

9. What is the agent's approach to editorial advice and career guidance for clients in general and the writer specifically?

10. How does the agent keep clients informed of his/her activities on their behalf? Does the agent send copies of publishers' rejection letters? Provide submission lists and rejection letters upon request? Send out updated activity reports regularly or upon request?

11. Does the agent consult with clients on any and all offers?

12. Some agencies sign subsidiary contracts on behalf of their clients to expedite processing. Does this agency?

13. What are the agent's commissions for basic sales to U.S. publishers; sales of movie and television rights; audio and multimedia rights; British and foreign translation rights.

14. What are the agents' procedures and time frames for processing and disbursing client funds? Does the agency keep different bank accounts, separating author funds from agency revenue?

15. What are the agent's policies about charging clients for expenses incurred by the agency? Will such expenses be listed? Does the agent advance money for such expenses? Does the agent consult with clients before advancing certain expenditures? Is there a ceiling on such expenses above which the agent will consult with clients?

16. How does the agent handle legal, accounting, public relations, or similar professional services that fall outside the normal range of a literary agency's functions?

17. Does the agency issue 1099 tax forms at the end of each year? Does it also furnish clients upon re-

quest with a detailed account of their financial activity, such as gross income, commissions, and other deductions, and net income, for the past year?

18. In the event of the agent's death or disability, or the death or disability of the principal person running the agency, what provisions exist for continuing operation of a writer's account, for the processing of money due to a writer, and for the handling of a writer's books and editorial needs?

19. If the agent and writer should part company, what is agency policy about handling any unsold subsidiary rights to the writer's work reserved under original publishing contracts?

20. What does the agent expect of the writer as a client? Does the agent have a list of Do's and Don'ts for clients that help writers help the agent do a better job?

SPELLING OUT THE TERMS

In the past, formal contracts between author and agent were rare; the final decision to work together might have been marked by no more than a handshake and a few words about commission rates. These days more and more agents ask their clients to sign an agreement outlining the responsibilities of each party. Occasionally the contract will cover a certain time period—three years, say, with the option to renew—but it's usually open-ended, and either party may cancel with reasonable advance notice. Such a contract is no substitute for trust, good will, and professional courtesy. Nor can it be relied on as an iron-clad safeguard: very rarely will either an agent or an author take the trouble (or incur the expense) of going to court to enforce a signed contract. Poets & Writers nonetheless recommends the use of some kind of written agreement, whether a formal contract or a rudimentary checklist (signed by both parties, a checklist has the same binding force as a contract).

Though the writer may argue that putting things in writing helps avoid misunderstandings, some agents won't like the idea; they may feel that the writer is betraying suspicion, that the crucial element of trust will be missing from the outset, that the author will make unreasonable demands. They may worry about the reaction of their other clients—should one author have a contract, however informal, if the others have none? A few agents may consider these points and refuse. A more common response will be relief: agents appreciate a writer with a businesslike attitude.

A checklist or other written agreement between author and agent should outline the scope of each party's responsibility to the other. Four broad topics need special attention: communication between agent and author; the types of work the agent will market; the disposition of rights; and continuing obligations should the relationship end.

Most literary agents are in New York, most writers are not; as a result, agent and author tend to communicate by letter or long-distance phone call. How often should they be in touch? What kind of news does the writer want to hear? If these questions seem too petty for serious contemplation, consider that countless writers grumble about the elusiveness of agents, and that agents, in private moments, are apt to complain about ceaseless pestering by anxious writers.

Some agents will want to handle all of a writer's work, no matter how short or how small the fee. Others will market only book-length manuscripts—the writer will have to peddle articles or short stories unassisted. Unless the writer is particularly prolific, a flexible, case-by-case arrangement usually works well.

A clear understanding of what rights, if any, the writer will *not* be assigning the agent is essential. Again, this may vary with each new manuscript, but if a general principle is stated at the outset, misunderstandings may be averted. The writer should also ask the agent about which rights he or she habitually sells to publishers, and which rights he or she likes to retain.

A contingency plan that faces squarely the possibility that the relationship may someday come to an end is actually in the best interest of both parties—neither the author nor the agent can know who, eventually, may want to leave whom.

A SAMPLE AGREEMENT

Following is a sample agency agreement one agent uses. Dated and addressed to the writer, it reads: This letter will confirm our Agreement as follows:

1. You hereby appoint me your sole and exclusive agent and representative for the marketing of all rights in your book proposal presently entitled ____ (the "Proposal") and any book you may hereafter write based upon it (the "Book").

2. I will render my services, attempting initially to market the Proposal to potential publishers of the Book. I will consult with you regarding submissions of the Proposal and advise you of all responses received.

3. You acknowledge that I have not given you assurances or guarantees that I will indeed be able to sell the Proposal and/or the Book to a publisher, but I will exert reasonable efforts to do so.

4. If I am able to obtain any offers for the publication of the Book, I will negotiate the terms of any such publication agreement on your behalf, subject to your approval, and you agree that I will be entitled to commission Fifteen Percent (15%) of the gross monies payable to you under any such agreement

into which you enter with a publisher in the United States. You agree that my standard agency clause,* a copy of which is attached, will be entered into any such publication agreement or, at the publisher's discretion, contained in a side letter between us relating to any such agreement.

5. You agree further that if you enter into a publication in accordance with the foregoing, I will thereafter continue to be your sole and exclusive agent for all rights in and to the Proposal and/or the Book (together, the "Work") which are not assigned to the publisher under the publication agreement (the "Reserved Subsidiary Rights").

6. I will exert reasonable efforts to market the Reserved Subsidiary Rights in the Work, but you acknowledge that I have not given you any assurances or guarantees that I will be able to sell any or all of the Reserved Subsidiary Rights on your behalf.

7. On any sales of any Reserved Subsidiary Rights in the United States which you agree to accept, I will be entitled to commission Fifteen Percent (15%) of the gross monies payable to you under any such agreements. On any sales of any of the Reserved

---

* Standard in book contracts negotiated by an agent, the agency clause confirms the agent as the writer's representative for that book and subsidiary rights the publisher sells for it.

Subsidiary Rights outside of the United States which you agree to accept, I will be entitled to commission Twenty Percent (20%) of the gross monies payable to you under any such agreements.

8. I will bear all expenses for postage, messengers, telephone and fax, and packaging for manuscripts that I incur in offering the Work to potential buyers of any and all rights. You agree to bear all expenses for postage, messengers, telephone and fax, and packaging for manuscripts that you incur in providing me with copies of the Work or in communicating with me and to reimburse me for any unusual expenses I may incur on your behalf at your specific request. You will, at your expense, initially provide me with two (2) clean photocopies of the Proposal, one of which I shall offer to publishers and one of which I shall retain in my office as a master copy. Notwithstanding the foregoing, should you and I agree, however, after consultation, to offer the Proposal in a simultaneous multiple submission requiring more than one offer copy, you will bear the cost of photocopying such additional offer copies as may be required for such agreed multiple submission. If the Book is sold to a publisher, upon its completion and acceptance you will provide me with such additional copies of the completed manuscript as may reasonably be required for my use in attempting to market the Reserved Subsidiary Rights in the Book.

9. You may terminate this Agreement by written notice to me upon the following terms and conditions:

a. Provided that at the time of such notice you have not entered into any publication agreement as a result of my efforts on your behalf under this Agreement; and

b. Provided that I will have a period of thirty (30) days from receipt of any such notice in which to send you a list of all submissions of the Work that I have made on your behalf which are still pending. If I provide you with such a list, you agree that if any publisher on that list subsequently makes an offer which you wish to accept, I will continue to act on your behalf as your agent and representative for the Work under the terms of this Agreement.

10. I may terminate this Agreement at any time by written notice to you.

11. You agree that prior to any termination of this agreement by either of us, you will not enter into any agency agreement with any other agent for any other proposal or book you may write without first providing me with a copy of any such other proposal or book and giving me an opportunity to discuss representing you in connection with such other proposal or book as well.

12. This Agreement does not constitute or acknowledge any partnership or joint venture between us.

13. This agreement constitutes the entire agreement between us with respect to the Work and no modification, amendment, waiver, or discharge or this Agreement or any provision of it, will be binding unless it is in writing and signed by us both.

Please indicate your agreement to the foregoing by signing in the space below.

THE NITTY-GRITTY

If the author and the agent agree to write out a checklist, here are some specific items they may want to discuss:

- The agency's commission rate for both domestic and foreign sales.

- The agent's right to a commission on work marketed by the author, for which the agent negotiates the contract; work the author markets and negotiates the contract for but which is officially represented by the agent; reprint permissions (these are usually sold not through the agent but through the publisher's permissions department).

- The author's involvement in mapping out the agent's sales pitch.

- The relative merits of exclusive submissions, multiple submissions, and auctions.

- The extent of the agent's duty as a first reader. Some encourage their clients to show them early drafts; others read only well-polished manuscripts.

- The extent of the agent's duty as watchdog over the publication process.

- The extent of the agent's duty as auxiliary publicist.

- What office expenses the agent will deduct from the writer's earnings.

- Which records the agent will keep.

- What personal information the agent may release about the author, and what information should be kept confidential.

An author's needs change as his or her career evolves; the agreement between author and agent should therefore be revised from time to time. With each new project, the author should also discuss specific marketing strategies and, once again, the disposition of specific rights.

RIGHTS FOR SALE

The total market value of a manuscript depends in part on the value of numerous subsidiary rights: film rights, TV rights, audio rights, translation rights, and so on. All these rights naturally belong to the author. But it is the agent's job, in consultation with the author, to decide what to sell when and to whom. Properly exploited, subsidiary rights can produce a handsome ancillary income. Agents earn commission on this income: 10 or 15 percent every time a subsidiary right is sold or optioned. They are therefore motivated to sell. Many good agents, in fact, thrive on the sale of subsidiary rights, especially movie and foreign rights.

Publishers are not unaware of the potential value of these rights, and when they negotiate to buy a book, they will typically try to pick up in the bargain whatever rights they can. Some rights are assigned to the hardcover publisher as a matter of course; the most important of these are trade and mass market paperback rights, and book club rights. To buy other rights, such as first serial, foreign, and audio, the publisher must offer a larger advance or some other inducement.

The publisher who snares a bundle of rights along with the manuscript is entitled to sell them to the highest bidder. The author is assigned a share of the proceeds of such sales (out of which the agent takes a commission). When reprint rights are sold, the publisher keeps half of the money and gives half back to the author. This division of spoils also applies to the reprint royalties—the hardcover publisher takes a bite out of the author's future earnings, too. If the publisher has bought first serial rights or dramatic rights, which is unusual but not unheard of, the split is 90/10 with the author receiving the lion's

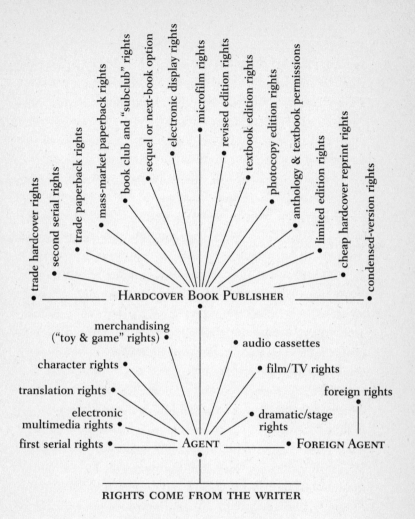

trade hardcover rights

second serial rights

trade paperback rights

mass-market paperback rights

book club and "subclub" rights

sequel or next-book option

electronic display rights

microfilm rights

revised edition rights

textbook edition rights

photocopy edition rights

anthology & textbook permissions

limited edition rights

cheap hardcover reprint rights

condensed-version rights

HARDCOVER BOOK PUBLISHER

merchandising
("toy & game" rights)

audio cassettes

character rights

film/TV rights

translation rights

foreign rights

electronic
multimedia rights

dramatic/stage
rights

first serial rights

AGENT ———— **FOREIGN AGENT**

RIGHTS COME FROM THE WRITER

Rights for Sale

This diagram shows the possibilities for a successful trade book.
The pattern does not hold true for every book; in fact, very few
realize their potential for all twenty-two uses.

share. The foreign rights split is generally 75/25, though UK rights may be split 80/20.

There's a catch here. When the hardcover publisher sells off various rights, the author's share of the proceeds is paid out only *after* the original advance has been re-couped. A brief example: an agent decides to give up the foreign rights to a novel when a publisher offers to buy world rights for $25,000. The publisher manages to ped-dle the novel in England, France, and Germany for a total of $12,000, of which $9,000 is due to the author on the basis of the 75/25 split. Not a penny will come to the author until the publisher has earned back the original $25,000 advance. If the book does well, the money will flow. But many books fail to "earn out," to use the pub-lisher's phrase, and the rights money never materializes.

Simple arithmetic makes it plain that the writer is better served by an agent who sells foreign rights directly to the foreign publisher, first serial rights directly to the magazine or newspaper, and so on. There are times when simple arithmetic is a poor guide to action—for example, when the publisher is better equipped than the agent to sell certain rights or when the author is desperate for cash up front—but otherwise, the numbers rule.

The agent has no choice but to sell trade and mass market paperback rights to the hardcover publisher, but there's room for negotiation. Some publishers offer what are called "hard/soft deals"—they propose a larger ad-vance in return for the right to print both hardcover and paperback editions. Agents like this kind of deal because it more or less guarantees a paperback edition and because the author receives a full royalty for every copy sold. The most common agreement, however, allows the hardcover publisher the option to sell reprint rights to another company.

These are tricky issues, complicated further by the uncertainty of any publishing effort. A good agent will explain the risks and potential benefits of selling and retaining various rights—and a responsible writer will pay close attention.

BREAKING UP IS HARD TO DO

When the author-agent relationship no longer works and the will to fix it has dissolved, it's time to get out. Too often, agent and author drift slowly apart, communication becomes strained and infrequent, both parties are unhappy, both hope for a change, but neither has the gumption to call it quits. This may sound like a certain kind of sour marriage, and indeed, the analogy extends still further: the eventual split can be messy, with enduring consequences, especially if over the years there have been many books together.

There are three common reasons for ending the relationship: the agent has been unable to sell the author's work and sees no point in making further attempts; the author is dissatisfied with the agent's efforts or attitude; or the author, having achieved a degree of success, wants a more powerful and diversified agency, lawyer, or both.

In the first case, the agent is responsible for signing

off in an honest, professional manner, and the writer for accepting the fact that not every partnership leads to success.

If the writer wishes to make a change, however, professional courtesy and practical considerations both require that the writer inform the agent of his or her decision *before* making a change. There's no point in adding insult to injury, or making an unfriendly break still more bitter; a forthright approach may smooth the negotiations that attend the dissolution of a partnership. In any event, a new agent won't represent a work until the old agent has clearly and willingly relinquished it.

Business dealings with the former agent are likely to continue. As mentioned earlier, an agent who negotiates a book contract continues to collect a commission on royalties due the author for as long as the contract remains in effect, whether or not the author is still a client. When the agent first negotiates the contract, certain rights attached to the work are relinquished to the publisher and others are retained by the agent in the author's name; unless agent and author sign an agreement that specifies otherwise, the agent has a legal right to a commission on the sale of any and all of those rights—even if the sale occurs after the agent has ceased to represent the author.

Say, for example, an agent sells a young author's first novel to a top editor at a major house. Though the agent works hard to get the best possible deal, the advance is modest; sales are, too, and the novel goes out of print. Fifteen years later, long after the author has changed agents and built a successful, lucrative career, a famous

Hollywood producer offers a hefty sum for the movie rights to the author's first novel. The agent, all but forgotten, who originally marketed that manuscript is legally entitled to a commission.

The writer who quits his or her agent can ask to withdraw any unsold rights. In many cases this request is granted, but not always. In short, it's a great deal easier to fire an agent when the agent was hired with care. A final stretch of the analogy: writers who present their agents with a "pre-nuptial" agreement find that divorce is less expensive.

CHAPTER FOUR

Selling Hard Copy in the Age of Cybertext: Agents and Authors Talk About the Business

Ask any writer and you'll probably hear at least one complaint about an agent: "He kept my manuscript for months without comment;" "She never returned my phone calls;" "He never let me know when my book had been turned down by one publisher and sent to another."

Talk to agents and you'll invariably hear about the dire straits of the publishing industry. Editors—even senior editors—have to fight for books they support. Some editors won't even look at a book unless it comes from two or three top agents. Mid-list fiction is a term of the past. The 5,000-book print run is a dead issue.

Sit down with editors and you'll hear their problems. Company policy forbids their reading unsolicited manuscripts—it's not cost-effective. All manuscripts must come by way of agents. Even then, the small, well-crafted novel has no chance against this season's blockbuster tell-all from the latest political hanger-on.

Before asking if anyone is having any fun here, let's go back to the agents. While some agents will consider unsolicited queries, almost none will read unsolicited manuscripts. Some agents didn't even want to be interviewed for a book like this.

But if a writer cannot get a book published without agency representation, if a writer needs to sell a work to an agent in order to sell it to a publisher, what is a writer to do?

"Go into another line of work?" suggested Liz Darhansoff of the Darhansoff & Verrill agency.

READERS ALL

Who are these agents, and how did they get into this line of work?

Ask a literary agent how he got into the business, and about half the time you'll hear, "I stumbled into it." And almost always you'll be told, "I had always loved to read. . . ."

"I stumbled into it by accident," says Richard Parks, 55, an independent agent since 1989. In the mid-1960s, "a friend's sister worked at the Curtis Brown agency, and her boss needed clerical help for the summer. By the end of the summer, I was hooked."

Parks, "always a reader," had majored in English at

Duke and had started teaching while doing graduate work in English at the University of North Carolina at Chapel Hill. But that summer, as he typed for one Curtis Brown agent, another staffer there asked for his help. She sat him down in front of a pile of mail. "Open Mr. Auden's mail," she ordered. "He's coming in this afternoon for it."

"I couldn't believe it," Parks says, still relishing the experience more than thirty years later. "There I was, *opening W. H. Auden's mail.* Curtis Brown represented writers I had read. I liked the work and the people, and I liked how my reading was connected to my work in a very direct way—different from teaching."

"I stumbled into it entirely by accident," says Henry Dunow, 44, an agent with Harold Ober Associates, Inc., for the last five years. "Though I've always been a reader, and at one point I even fancied myself a writer. My father was a Yiddish writer.

"Right after college, in the early 1970s, I worked for Harper & Row as an editorial assistant. After that I vowed never to work in publishing or to have any kind of a straight nine-to-five job again. I went to California to act, then came back to New York and worked in the theater."

A "struggling out-of-work actor," Dunow answered an ad in *The New York Times* and "was hired as an agent at a horrid place I won't name. I worked there briefly, then went to Curtis Brown. It was an extremely ironic surprise to stumble back into the business, but it makes sense. I grew up in a home where a writer was taken care of, so it's more than mere coincidence that I take care of writers now. And I have an added empathy for struggling artists because as an actor, I was always looking for better representation."

"Books and music are my two loves," says Joseph Regal, 28, an agent with Russell & Volkening. "I sang professionally and I'm still in a band. But I needed a real job, so I called a friend at Random House. She said, 'Do you want to be an agent or an editor?' I didn't know.

"Russell & Volkening was my first interview. Tim Seldes [the owner] said I would get a better overview of the business as an agent than as an editor, so I committed to a couple of years."

Regal has now been with Russell & Volkening for six years. "I got very lucky," he says of stumbling into the business. "I feel a lot of pride working for writers like Anne Tyler and Nadine Gordimer."

Other agents started in publishing. Seldes, proprietor of Russell & Volkening, began as managing editor of the trade division of Doubleday & Co. in 1948. He moved up the publishing management ladder, but chucked it all in 1972 to become an agent so he could own his own business.

Liz Darhansoff, now in her early fifties, started as a publicist at Atheneum in 1966, then moved on to Random House. In 1973 she went to work as an agent for International Creative Management, one of the top bicoastal agencies out of New York City. "I wanted to be at the beginning of the publishing process, not the end," she says. "Being a publicist is hard—if the book is successful, you get no credit. If it fails, you get all the blame. It's a burn-out job." Darhansoff stayed at ICM for two years before opening her own agency. "I wanted to do the books I wanted to do—not what was necessary to keep a big agency afloat."

Chuck Verrill joined the group about three years ago, and with agent Leigh Feldman, a bookkeeper and a support staff of two, the agency now represents about 150 authors.

Expanding on her earlier remark, Darhansoff says, "Not a whole lot comes from blind queries. People who are serious about their writing should know how to find a recommendation for it. They research who might like the work, they get it read and recommended to an agent."

Despite the fact agents agree blind queries yield little that is publishable, the queries never stop. Darhansoff & Verrill receives 50 to 100 such queries a week, or 26,000 to 52,000 a year. "Most writers obey the rules and don't send the manuscript," she notes.

Most of her clients come from recommendations. For example, Darhansoff came to represent E. Annie Proulx from an editor's recommendation. Darhansoff has also represented author Lee Smith since 1976, and through her she has found a lot of southern clients.

Then there's the people she knows in the business. Darhansoff had known William Kennedy since she was a publicist and he was a book reviewer for the Albany (NY) *Times Union*. When she became an agent, Kennedy sent several writers her way over the years, "until one day he said, " 'What about me?' " Darhansoff has represented his work since *Ironweed*, including the successful paperback republishing of his earlier novels.

If agents have a mantra for writers these days, it's

- Do your research, and

- Write, don't call.

"Use your network," adds Henry Dunow. "Think of editors, writers, teachers you know. At the very least, address your query to a particular individual at an agency. If you don't know anyone at that agency, call and ask the receptionist whom to address your query to. Ask what kind of work the agents handle."

Dunow, an agent for twelve years, working at the Ober agency for five, sees only letters addressed to him personally—including half a dozen queries a day, or more than 1,000 a year. He estimates the agency as a whole, with three agents and one junior agent, receives about a dozen queries a day.

Into the slush pile go letters addressed "Dear Mr. Ober," since Harold Ober died in the 1950s, and those addressed "Dear Sir." And one year *Literary Market Place* misspelled Dunow's surname in its agents' listing. "So when I receive a letter addressed to Mr. Durkow, I know I've been chosen at random," he says, and the query goes to the bottom of the pile.

In the mid 1980s, when he was working for Curtis Brown, Ltd., Dunow went to the Iowa Writers Workshop to make contacts with writers. "I took on a number of writers from Iowa who have served as a continuing center of a network," he says, including Mary Gaitskill and William Kotzwinkle.

"When I started as an agent I felt there must be a great secret to finding clients," he adds, "but there's no particular rhyme or reason to it. It's a matter of critical mass. The list continues to build."

Independent agent Richard Parks has found new clients through query letters, but they tend to be writers of nonfiction. He gets an "overwhelming" 50 to 75 queries a week "and the sad truth is I can't consider them all." Most of his new clients come through referrals.

"We occasionally take on writers who come through the mail, but author recommendations are more productive," says Joe Regal. "Writers who are working hard become part of a community. If they meet some writers, have some talent, they'll find a way to break in."

If a writer must come in over the transom, how should she arrive?

Presentation is vital, if not all. No "Dear Agent" or "Dear Sir" letters, of course. No wrinkled paper, no misspelled words.

But beyond that, rewriting applies to a query letter just as much as it does to a book. Says Regal, "A writer has to know how to grab a reader, whether writing a book or a query letter. What appeals to the reader in either is intuitive—the breakdown of sentences, the flow of the language. What is good writing, after all?"

Whatever it is, your query letter had better have it.

"An author will say, 'My query letter's no good, but take a look at my book,' " says Regal. "It doesn't work that way."

Jean Naggar, something of a legend in the field for finding gold in the hills of the slush pile, was the only agent Poets & Writers talked to who acknowledged the mail as productive.

"I am still finding new writers through unsolicited queries," says Naggar, who burst onto the high stakes literary scene twenty years ago with the discovery of Jean Auel's *The Clan of the Cave Bear*. "My criterion is not who the writer knows, but what the query is like."

Note that Naggar, an agent since 1978, refers to unsolicited *queries,* not manuscripts. She promises a query turnaround of twenty-four hours, but if she is not interested in the proposal, she will not say why. "Perhaps I just don't like it—that's a subjective opinion that could be harmful to a writer."

If she is interested, she will ask for sample chapters, nothing more, which she will read within a week. If she is still interested, she will ask to see the entire book, and then a writer must be patient.

"It takes a long time to get a reading," Naggar says frankly. "Two to six months, depending on how many manuscripts I have from writers who are already clients—they take precedence. And I now have a lot of writers writing," she adds, noting that she and two other agents represent 140 writers.

Like other agents, Naggar reads a full manuscript only on exclusive—no shopping the manuscript around while she is considering it. "The manuscript gets serious attention here—it's read by two of us—and I don't charge a fee."

Naggar does not make notes as she reads. "It's more how the book strikes me as a whole, though I may give some specifics." And if she turns down a manuscript, she does not usually say why. She comments only "if I am prepared to put myself on the line for a writer. It's not my job or responsibility to send back a full report, which a lot of writers seem to expect."

Naggar's agency receives 5,000 queries a year, she says, and after twenty years, clients whose first books she sold now have as many as fourteen books published. "The workload has grown exponentially," she notes, "and I have far less room for new commitments."

AN ADVOCACY RELATIONSHIP

Once an agency finds a writer, it seldom offers a contract.

Henry Dunow represents between 40 and 50 writers. "I've always worked at agencies that went on a handshake," he says. "This is an advocacy relationship, not an adversarial one. You work together as long as it's productive.

"I don't fire clients, ever," he adds, "but inevitably some people become less active or we drift apart. If it's not working, all it takes is a phone call."

Russell & Volkening, founded in 1940, has worked with its writers on a verbal handshake ever since. "It's better for us both," says Regal. "On my side, I know I need to do my best to keep the author happy and make his career happen. And an author who's unhappy shouldn't have to stick around. In my six years here, there has been only one situation where there was perhaps too much of a gray area. In general, if you're honorable, people are honorable back. With rare exceptions, our authors are easy to deal with and very professional."

Large agencies, such as International Creative Management or William Morris, use contracts. Liz Darhansoff commits to her clients one book at a time.

Jean Naggar and Richard Parks both use letters of agreement. "It defines my responsibilities and duties," says Naggar, whose agreement was drawn up by a lawyer client several years ago. "It's fair to the writer and myself and good for consciousness-raising, if nothing else."

Parks has a letter of agreement he uses "if the author wants. In many instances, they don't—they're friends of current clients who are happy. But if a writer wants it, I have a simple agreement that spells out my responsibilities." Nothing more. "If a writer's not happy, it's silly to try to tie him to me with a contract," says Parks, who currently represents between 30 and 35 writers.

Since 1989, he can recall only one instance where the relationship didn't work. "A young writer, in graduate school, got mad at me because I sent copies of rejection letters with a note about where I would send the book next. He thought I wasn't sympathetic enough. But I can't remember any major blow-ups."

The general exception to this feeling of trust is the agency clause that agents put in every book contract they sell, making them the agent for that book and everything that happens to it, even if they are no longer the agent for its writer.

WAXES AND WANES

"If it's not working, all it takes is a phone call" covers a fairly vast desert of complex feelings and relationships.

"Agents are human beings," observes one writer with twenty-five years experience in the business. "They have their waxes and wanes, like anyone else. I was represented for several years by a very good agent. When she started to turn my fiction over to her assistant, I felt I couldn't object, because I hadn't been earning the agency (or myself) much money. But neither did I feel that her assistant was representing me well, and she wasn't the agent I had chosen.

"The assistant sent some stories of mine to major magazines, but she didn't really seem to think about them, or their market. At my urging she reluctantly sent a story to a major general interest magazine, which published it, bringing me national exposure, lots of nice letters and money, too. My agent refused to send another story to that magazine, saying it wasn't my best work, but let me send it to my editor there. The editor liked it very much and the magazine almost bought it.

"In short, I began to think this agent was no longer my best reader. On the one hand, that's life, and I accept it; on the other, it was very discouraging. And because the agent and I have never officially parted company, I feel—and this has been confirmed by another, honorable agent—that I would have to give her first refusal of my next book. When that time comes, I guess I'll just deal with it. If the agent wants to really push the book, great; if she's just going to hand it over to her assistant, no dice.

"Of course, I won't be that blunt; I'm the world's biggest coward."

PARTNERSHIP

Whether or not an agent will submit short stories, and where she'll submit them, is something to talk about up-front, and as the partnership continues, as necessary.

Partnership is another key word here. Prolific short story writer and novelist Stephen Dixon of Baltimore, Maryland, handled and placed all his own work for fifteen years. "I'm a great letter writer," he says. "I would work my way in, and I had small press publications to list. I was satisfied. I didn't want someone peering over my shoulder and trying to make my work more commercial. But now I feel independent—I'm known, my work is known and people take it as it is."

In 1992 Dixon agreed to have most of his fiction represented by Witherspoon Associates. The agency negotiates book and subsidiary rights contracts for him, and Dixon sells his short stories to magazines. "The agency didn't handle my stories when they first took me on. Then I sold two to *Harper*'s and they said, 'We can do that!' So for two years they handled my stories, and for a year and a half they didn't sell one of them. I would take one or two back at a time, and place them.

"Finally I gave them a month's notice, saying as of January 1, 1997, I would handle my own stories. I just talked to the editor of the *Ohio Journal*, which is accepting a story. I can deal with magazine editors as well as the agency can."

Dixon, who teaches in the writing program at Johns Hopkins University, had published fourteen books and about 500 short stories without a literary agent. Why fix something that apparently wasn't broken?

"What changed my mind was that the contracts got more complicated and I had difficulty with a publisher," he says. Dixon's novel *Frog* was nominated for a National Book Award right before it was published in 1991. The book sold out immediately, says Dixon, but its publisher, British American, did not reprint it.

"When I said I wanted the rights back, they printed 1,000 more. They sold those, went out of business and gave me back the rights," says Dixon.

Dixon met Kim Witherspoon at a dinner honoring NBA nominees. She wrote to him later, he says, suggesting that Allen Peacock, an editor at Holt, might be interested in his work.

When *Frog* was nominated for a PEN/Faulkner Award, Dixon met Peacock at the awards ceremony. Dixon recalls their conversation.

"Allen said, 'If you ever want to leave British American. . . .' "

"I said, 'Take me, I'm yours.' "

"He said, 'What have you got?' "

"I said, 'Sixty to seventy pages and an idea for a collection of interconnected short stories.' "

Peacock was interested, and although Dixon felt he had made the contact himself, "I thought, Why do this myself? Kim told me Allen was interested in my work and she may have talked me up to him.

"I figured I wouldn't lose any money by having an agent, and I would be better protected. Even Allen said I would be better off with an agent."

The agency options his work for movies and handles foreign rights sales, work Dixon formerly did himself. But when his novel *Too Late*, long out of print, was sold for a film in France, "the contract was so complicated, I asked Kim for help. Their sub-agent in France did a very good job of negotiating it.

"I teach, I take care of my family and I write," he says. "Even simple contracts became onerous. Sometimes I feel I have lost some control," Dixon acknowledges. "I have to abide by certain proprieties now, a certain protocol, that I didn't use to. My work used to appear all over the place. But Holt is the first major publisher to publish more than two of my books."

And his work still appears widely, not confined to any one publisher or form.

"I'm still not making any money," says Dixon. "In 1978 I got a $3,000 advance for *Too Late* from Harper & Row [without an agent]. In the 1990s I got a $10,000 advance for each of three books from Holt. The publisher still feels it's taking a chance on me, and the works aren't block-busters. I'm still just grateful to be published."

ALTERNATE ROUTES

Agents will in some cases, for some clients, represent books that are from the start noncommercial, but they are not necessarily specifically looking for these kinds of books.

"I quite often submit work to independent presses or university presses, though I don't take such work at the outset, if that's the obvious direction it's going in," says Henry Dunow. "Agents can just clog up the works with a smaller press—they're less effective and necessary—and at a university press, an agent can be potentially obstructive to a sale. Quite often if no major trade house is interested in a book, I will take it elsewhere."

As an example, he cites Robert Hellenga's first novel, *The Sixteen Pleasures*. "I represented that book for five years. We received forty rejections from the finest literary editors. Then I sold it to SoHo Press for a modest four-figure advance. My feeling was one of resignation that the book would not make a difference in the writer's life or mine."

Not so. "SoHo Press did a brilliant job" of publishing *The Sixteen Pleasures*, says Dunow. "They put it in the forefront of the list. It got much more attention than it would have at a big house, and got fabulous critical reviews."

Film rights and some foreign rights were sold. Dell brought paperback rights for six figures "and did very well with it," says Dunow.

Liz Darhansoff also says she has placed "a lot" of work with smaller publishers. Her client Jill McCorkle "was practically the first writer Algonquin published. They're old-fashioned, wonderful to work with. So is Workman— they start modestly, but they're creative and never let a book fail. They have a good time, and I love working with them."

"A quality writer will find a way to publication," says Dunow. "The system works to that extent. At the same time, "particularly in literary fiction, the 'serious but quiet' book was easier to sell seven or eight years ago."

AND MORE PARTNERSHIP

Writers with a novel that cannot easily be categorized, or a collection of short stories, should especially be prepared to work in partnership with an agent, should they have one.

Tom Perotta of Cambridge, Massachusetts finished *Bad Haircut: Stories of the '70s* in 1990. The collection consisted of ten connected stories, three of which had been published in literary magazines. Kim Witherspoon of Witherspoon Associates represented him and "she submitted the book quite aggressively," he says. "But publishers were skittish then about short story collections, in a way they hadn't been in the eighties. The reaction was,

'We're very interested, but we're not doing short stories by an unknown author. We'd love to see a novel.' "

Perotta and Witherspoon agreed she would submit, instead, a novel he had finished in the meantime, and he would send the short story collection to contests and small presses.

For the next two years, Witherspoon submitted the novel to thirty publishers without getting a bite. The short story collection was a finalist in the Drue Heinz and Associated Writing Programs contests, without winning a prize.

"Despair is too strong a word," says Perotta. "But I felt I had two good books and no publisher."

Then a friend of his who read manuscripts for a new publisher, Bridgeworks, in Bridgehampton, New York, heard that *Bad Haircut* had been an AWP contest finalist. She asked Perotta to send it on, and Bridgeworks accepted it.

"It wasn't published until 1994," says Perotta, "but then the book took on a life of its own, with success on a scale I had never hoped for." *Bad Haircut* sold 4,000 copies in hardcover and 25,000 copies as a mass-market paperback from Berkley. "That's a remarkable life for the kind of book it is, and it propelled me as a writer to a different level."

After Berkley's relative success with *Bad Haircut*, Witherspoon showed Perotta's second novel, *Election*, to G. P. Putnam. "It's a short novel, a little peculiar, set in high school," says Perotta. "They said, 'Let us think about it for later.' "

Another well-connected friend of Perotta's put him in touch with a movie producer who optioned *Election*. That interested Putnam, though by then (1996) they had bought Perotta's third novel, *The Wishbones*, based on three chapters. Fox 2000 had optioned *The Wishbones* for a movie in what Perotta describes as "a much more formal process" than his first movie option. A West Coast agency represented the book, and a producer and screenwriter were lined up. Putnam decided to publish *The Wishbones* in 1997 and scheduled *Election* for 1998.

His first novel has never been published.

The first key to his success, he says, is "I was able to keep writing during that period that paralyzes most writers."

The second is, "I think it would be a mistake to think that this life—contracts, movie deals—was real life." Perotta teaches fiction writing in the summer creative writing program at Yale and expository writing at Harvard.

Further, he points out, "*Election* and *Bad Haircut* were years between writing and publication, while *Wishbones* was bought from three chapters and published quickly. There's no reason to believe a good book will be published promptly or recognized quickly."

Perotta talks about the "collaborative effort" between him and his agent. "A lot of the opportunities for my books I created on my own. But the agent helped me capitalize on them, and gave me good advice every step of the way, so I made no missteps."

Over the years of his submissions, Perotta, now 35, learned that he likes "a personal comfort with an agent, someone I can talk to a fair amount. But I know people vary widely." For that reason, he and Kim Witherspoon agreed at one point that Perotta would be more comfortable represented by another agent in the firm, Maria Massie. "[In 1996] I talked with Maria almost weekly, just chatting, or going over details of the several contracts in process. I like to be able to do that."

Witherspoon Associates is very good with foreign rights sales, says Perotta, and is connected with the Creative Artists Agency for film projects.

"I tend to hang onto my work until it's highly polished, so I'm not looking for editing from an agent. So I hadn't realized, and I think a lot of writers don't, what agents can do. It may look as though an agent does little or does what you could do yourself—send manuscripts to editors. But after the basic sale, agents can capitalize on other opportunities in a way a writer working alone can't. They know agents in other countries, film scouts and film producers. And a movie deal is much more complicated than a book contract.

"The publishing market is difficult now," he adds. "Witherspoon Associates had invested in me for four years before I made a penny. But a lot of my early success came outside the standard publishing structure.

"I've noticed a lot more writers having their first book published with a small press, and getting as much attention as a mid-list book would, buried in a catalogue with hundreds of other commercial press books."

Perotta is now back to writing short stories. "It's hard work," he says, and he still has a tough time getting them published. He submits the stories to magazines himself. "It seems only fair—there isn't much money involved and I'd rather have the agency focus on bigger things." Short story writers have to be as resourceful as poets, he advises. "You have to go down every path. And don't be surprised if an agent won't represent your work—don't take it as a black mark against your work."

FEEDBACK

Submitting manuscripts to editors and then capitalizing on the opportunities for that manuscript seem to be an agent's main duties these days. When it comes to editing a client's manuscript or just giving feedback, they take their cue from the writer.

"It's up to the writer and the writer's needs," says Richard Parks. "For some I do a lot, while others bring in polished material ready to go. In some cases I might have to do more than I used to because editors are caught up in the world of corporate publishing and no longer have time to actually edit. More often I serve as a reliable mirror, saying, 'Look at this,' or, 'This is a bad spot here.' "

"One of the most interesting and motivating aspects of being an agent is being close to the creation of a work," says Henry Dunow. "So I don't do line editing so much as talk about concepts, structure, pacing—that kind of feedback. I work very closely with authors of nonfiction on their proposals, because those are selling tools," he adds. "With fiction, I need it, if not in its final polished state, then in a form in which I can effectively sell it."

When working with a manuscript, these agents still think of hard copy. Of the half-dozen agents Poets & Writers talked to, only Richard Parks, who works in a home office, was wholeheartedly "online," logging on every morning at 7:30 and communicating with clients via E-mail.

"On a day-to-day level, it's the greatest invention in a long time," says Parks. "Yes, sometimes it's too easy, but if you're disciplined, it's a big help. I'm old enough to remember when an agent didn't make a long-distance call except for something *very* important, and if an agent had to return a writer's long-distance call, the writer was charged for the call.

"Now I use the phone as if every call were local," and snail mail is too slow.

In contrast, "My IBM Selectric is still all I need," says Henry Dunow. As of 1996, Harold Ober Associates had set up what Dunow referred to as "a limited network." Perhaps it is something like the one in Jean Naggar's office. "Lots of writers E-mail us," she says, "but we have only one computer that can receive it. I much prefer a letter, call, or fax in any case, though we give the fax number only to clients."

"I get hammered by our authors because we aren't networked outside the office," says Joe Regal, who had recently overseen the setting up of a network within Russell & Volkening. "But I promise you, by the time this book comes out, we'll be networked with the rest of the world."

"We have E-mail, but I don't encourage it," says Liz Darhansoff. "A client in Connecticut wanted us to wire his money so we did, and it wound up in the Boston branch of his Connecticut bank, in someone else's account. I said to him, 'Remember when I used to keep a ledger?'"

Electronic publishing seems to be something agents worry about, if nothing else. Noting that being an agent these days is "wildly different" from his nine years with Curtis Brown in the 1970s, Parks cites the burgeoning of electronic publishing as one of the major differences. "It's a big issue in publishing contracts, particularly for writers who do a lot of magazine work. What rights the writer keeps or doesn't keep is a thorny issue, in part just because we don't know how valuable electronic publishing will be or where it will go."

While CDs are "yesterday's news," electronic adaptations are another problem, he says, "because the movie companies want them, so they don't want the publishers to have them."

Agents, caught in the middle of all this, are "scrambling to keep up with what's happening in the field—we don't want to regret something down the road," says Parks. The Association of Authors' Representatives is trying to help its member agents avoid that regret. Parks, an AAR board member, is also board liaison with the AAR Electronic Media Committee. "We all feel we must keep up on this, so, for example, we bring in experts to keep us informed."

"In twenty-five years," predicts Joe Regal, "everyone

will have access to the Internet one way or the other, and publishers won't be the choice for a certain kind of book anymore. They'll be more the imprimatur of good taste."

Right now, he points out, for certain kinds of niche nonfiction, a reader can go on the Internet, do a search and find a web site for that subject or group without ever buying a book. Or, an author can research a subject, get a web site, keyboard a book onto it, and take orders. "The author will sell maybe half as many copies as he might with a hard copy book, but he'll make four times the money as he would with royalties," says Regal.

Other kinds of nonfiction are particularly suited to publication both electronically and in hard copy. For example, Fred Goodman's *The Mansion on the Hill / Dylan, Young, Geffen, Springsteen and the Head-On Collision of Rock and Commerce*, first appeared in serial form on the Internet, says Regal. "This makes sense—you could hear some of the music and the interviews on your computer speakers."

Fiction, however, cannot happen that way, he says. "There's a lot of writing posted on the Internet right now, but it's not very good, and people want to read good stuff." That's where the publisher comes in. Publishers like Farrar, Straus & Giroux, Algonquin, or Bridgeworks "sift through the stuff in a way the net doesn't."

For the last two or three years, Russell & Volkening has fought the "electronic battle," says Regal, agreeing with Parks, "We have to protect our authors, since we don't know what will happen with this." Yet in early 1997, the scene seemed to be changing. There was still no electronic publishing to speak of, and some CD-ROM companies were already downsizing. "Even our best-known authors are not online," says Regal.

THE BOOK WILL SURVIVE

For years pundits have predicted stories would live, but the book as an entity, would die, but the book has not died. As the industry races toward the third millenium, the agents decry the state of publishing but not the state of the book.

"It's much harder to get a literary novelist published today, and that's my stock in trade," says Joe Regal. "Twenty years ago, literary novelists didn't make money any more than they do today, for their first or third or fifth book, but they were still published because of their merit." And a publisher could be rewarded for that faith —Regal cites Knopf and Anne Tyler. "Her first six novels probably didn't sell 50,000 copies total," he says. "But she was building a loyal readership."

The agents agreed publishers will take a chance on a writer's first book—"you never know if something will be a hit," says Regal. But they won't take chances after that. "It's terrible for the industry, incredibly short-sighted," says Regal, "and it's accelerated in the last five years."

"There is still a strong [publishing] market for young, new literary fiction," says Richard Parks, "but the sad truth is, if after three or four books, that writer hasn't 'hit,' then that writer is out. We're losing a lot of good things in no longer publishing 'mid-list' fiction, but the fact is we've lost a lot of readers." He takes some heart in the trend he sees of older writers "reinventing themselves by turning to nonfiction or category fiction," which he calls a "crowded field, but still viable."

"Publishing reflects the larger world," says Henry Dunow. "The explosion of media and the communications industry, the whole culture subjected to mass-marketing, which has an effect on television programs, films, and books.

"The result is publishers are guided by a big-book mentality, the after-effect of more than ten years of corporate conglomeratization. The five-thousand print run is a dead issue."

Then the question arises, Is anyone here having any fun?

"I think so," says Richard Parks. "You tend to hear about the bad stuff. But when you find some wonderful, young new voice, and you see the writer's life change with the publication of her book—that's exciting."

"Yes," says Liz Darhansoff firmly, adding that while the situation looks bleak, she has also been in the business long enough to see things cyclically. She mentions the publishers she likes working with, like Algonquin and Workman—"they're wonderful and creative and have a good time. I also love working with Faith Sale at Putnam, Carol Smith at Norton and Dan Frank at Pantheon. I may be dealing more with corporations, but I'm still working with editors. There are frustrations, and satisfactions, too."

"I'm having fun," says Henry Dunow. "The work is a good fit to my talents, interests, and limitations. It's always interesting, and the days go by fast, full of challenges, along with some anxiety and frustration. I don't want to sound too lofty," he adds. "I recognize a strong marketing angle in a book. But I don't want to sound too cynical either—I'm still drawn to the quality of the sentences. The motivating common denominator in my choice of books to represent is strong writing."

Joe Regal is having fun. "An agent is one-third lawyer, one-third editor and one-third schmoozer, with a little bit of psychologist thrown in. I'm never bored—in any one day, I might be conducting a book auction, handling motion picture rights, or working with an author, editing a manuscript, or helping with another problem.

"This is a rough time in publishing, but there are lessons to be learned, and if publishers learn them—and they have to—we'll be in a golden age. More people read books today than have ever read. Yes, they read John Grisham mysteries and books about their computers, but this is a potentially good time that publishers have not yet adjusted to."

"I'm trying to pull back, but it's hard," says Jean Naggar. "I still love the thrill of the find."

"We go forth, unafraid," says Tim Seldes, recalling his prep school motto.

LITERARY AGENCIES: AN ANNOTATED LIST

The 120 literary agencies listed here will consider unsolicited—that is, unreferred—material without charging a reading fee. In almost all cases these agents want to see queries and proposals first, *not* complete manuscripts, and they much prefer mail queries over telephone queries.

These agents are all members of the Association of Authors' Representatives, Inc., formed in 1991 through the merger of the Society of Authors' Representatives (founded in 1928) and the Independent Literary Agents Association (founded in 1977). AAR member agents meet professional standards specified in the organization's bylaws and agree to subscribe to its eight-point canon of ethics. This canon includes not charging reading fees and keeping separate bank accounts for client and agency funds.

Always, always enclose a self-addressed, stamped envelope when writing to an agent. Material sent without an SASE will most often be discarded without a reply.

Writers may want to note that most agents consider a "reading" and an "evaluation" as two quite separate tasks. A manuscript turned down by an agent will most likely come back with nothing more than a polite "no thanks." This is partly because an agent does not have time to comment on rejected manuscripts, but also because personal taste and market realities play a large part in an agent's decision. As one agent said, "If I don't want to represent a manuscript, it doesn't mean it's not good."

Many agencies do not charge for any services. At others, clients may be required to reimburse the agency for expenses such as long-distance telephone calls, photocopying, and postage. Usually these reimbursements are paid only after the agent makes a sale.

This list was compiled from questionnaires Poets & Writers, Inc., sent to the 290 AAR member agents. Two hundred sixteen agents responded, and 120 of those agreed to be listed in this book.

Carole Abel Literary Agency
160 West 87th Street
New York, NY 10024
Phone: (212) 724-1168   Fax: (212) 724-1384

Contact: Carole Abel

Agency Commission: 15%   Abroad: 25%

Categories Represented: Fiction and nonfiction, biographies, health, new age, cookbooks. No children's, poetry, science fiction, horror, or screenplays.

Phone Queries: Y   Unsolicited Mss: N
Mail Queries: Y   Poetry Collections: N
SASE: Y

Bret Adams Limited
448 West 44th Street
New York, NY 10036
Phone: (212) 765-5630   Fax: (212) 265-2212

Contact: Bruce Ostler

Agency Commission: 10%   Abroad: 20%

Categories Represented: Plays and screenplays. No literature, novels, poetry, short stories, or nonfiction.

Phone Queries: N   Unsolicited Mss: N
Mail Queries: Y   Poetry Collections: N
SASE: Y

Miriam Altshuler Literary Agency
RR#1, Box 5
Red Hook, NY 12571
Phone: (914) 758-9408   Fax: (914) 758-3118

Contact: Miriam Altshuler

Agency Commission: 15%   Abroad: 20%

Categories Represented: Literary, commercial fiction and nonfiction. No romance, Westerns, or science fiction.

Phone Queries: N   Unsolicited Mss: N
Mail Queries: Y   Poetry Collections: N
SASE: Y

IMG - Julian Bach Literary Agency
22 East 71st Street
New York, NY 10021
Phone: (212) 772-8900   Fax: (212) 772-2617

Contact: Carolyn Krupp

Agency Commission: 15%   Abroad: 20%

Categories Represented: Mainstream and literary fiction, nonfiction, self-help.

Phone Queries: N   Unsolicited Mss: N
Mail Queries: Y   Poetry Collections: N
SASE: Y

The Balkin Agency, Inc.
317 South Pleasant Street
Amherst, MA 01002
Phone: (413) 256-1934   Fax: (413) 256-1935

Contact: Richard Balkin

Agency Commission: 15%   Abroad: 20%

Categories Represented: Adult nonfiction, reference, college text.

Phone Queries: N   Unsolicited Mss: N
Mail Queries: Y   Poetry Collections: N
SASE: Y

Comments: "My favorites are American history, popular culture, science, natural history, biography, film."

Virginia Barber Literary Agency
101 Fifth Avenue
New York, NY 10003
Phone: (212) 255-6515   Fax: (212) 691-9418

Contact: Virginia Barber, Jennifer Rudolph Walsh, Jay Mandel, Cornelius Howland, Claire Tisne

Agency Commission: Not specified

Categories Represented: Specialize in literary fiction and nonfiction. No poetry, children's, or illustrated.

Phone Queries: N   Unsolicited Mss: N
Mail Queries: Y   Poetry Collections: N
SASE: Y

Berman, Boals & Flynn, Inc.
225 Lafayette Street
Suite 1207
New York, NY 10012
Phone: (212) 966-0339

Contact: Judy Boals

Agency Commission: 10%   Abroad: 10%

Categories Represented: Plays and a few screenplays
only. No books, manuscripts, or novels.

Phone Queries: N   Unsolicited Mss: N
Mail Queries: Y   Poetry Collections: N
SASE: Y

Meredith Bernstein Literary Agency
2112 Broadway
Suite 503-A
New York, NY 10023
Phone: (212) 799-1007   Fax: (212) 799-1145

Contact: Meredith Bernstein, Elizabeth Cavanaugh

Agency Commission: 15%   Abroad: 10%

Categories Represented: All kinds of fiction and non-fiction. No juveniles, screenplays, or poetry.

Phone Queries: N   Unsolicited Mss: N
Mail Queries: Y   Poetry Collections: N
SASE: Y

Pam Bernstein & Associates, Inc.
790 Madison Avenue
Suite 310
New York, NY 10021
Phone: (212) 288-1700   Fax: (212) 288-3054
E-mail: pbernassoc@aol.com

Contact: Pam Bernstein, Donna Dever

Agency Commission: 15%   Abroad: 20%

Categories Represented: Women's fiction and nonfiction, psychology, spiritual, self-help, consumer issues. No children's, poetry, short stories, or horror.

Phone Queries: N   Unsolicited Mss: N
Mail Queries: Y   Poetry Collections: N
SASE: Y

Vicky Bijur Literary Agency
333 West End Avenue
Suite 5B
New York, NY 10023
Phone: (212) 580-4108   Fax: (212) 496-1572

Contact: Vicky Bijur, Clarissa Hulton

Agency Commission: 15%   Abroad: 20%

Categories Represented: Fiction, primarily in the mystery genre, nonfiction, all types. No Romance.

Phone Queries: N   Unsolicited Mss: N
Mail Queries: Y   Poetry Collections: N
SASE: Y

Comments: Fax queries not accepted.

David Black Literary Agency, Inc.
156 Fifth Avenue
Suite 608
New York, NY 10010
Phone: (212) 242-5080   Fax: (212) 924-6609

Contact: Gary Morris, Susan Raihofer

Agency Commission: 15%   Abroad: 20%

Categories Represented: Serious nonfiction, politics, sports, and commercial fiction.

Phone Queries: N   Unsolicited Mss: N
Mail Queries: Y   Poetry Collections: N
SASE: Y

Georges Borchardt, Inc.

136 East 57th Street
New York, NY 10022
Phone: (212) 753-5785   Fax: (212) 838-6518

Contact: Georges Borchardt, Anne Borchardt, Denise Shannon

Agency Commission: 15%   Abroad: 20%

Categories Represented: Literary fiction and first rate nonfiction.

Phone Queries: N   Unsolicited Mss: N
Mail Queries: Y   Poetry Collections: N
SASE: Y

Comments: Mail queries accepted only from authors recommended by agency contacts.

Brandt & Brandt Literary Agents, Inc.

1501 Broadway
New York, NY 10036
Phone: (212) 840-5760   Fax: (212) 840-5776

Contact: Carl D. Brandt, Gail Hochman, Marianne Merola, Charles Schlessinger

Agency Commission: 15%   Abroad: 20%

Categories Represented: None specified.

Phone Queries: N
Mail Queries: Y
SASE: Y

Unsolicited Mss: N
Poetry Collections: N

Broadway Play Publishing
56 East 81st Street
New York, NY 10028-0202
Phone: (212) 772-8334   Fax: (212) 772-8358
E-mail: broadwaypl@aol.com

Contact: Christopher Gould

Agency Commission: 10-20%

Categories Represented: Original, contemporary, full-length American plays only.

Phone Queries: Y
Mail Queries: Y
SASE: Y

Unsolicited Mss: N
Poetry Collections: N

Andrea Brown Literary Agency, Inc.
P.O. Box 429
El Cranada, CA 94018
Phone: (415) 728-1783

Contact: Andrea Brown

Agency Commission: 15%   Abroad: 20%

Categories Represented: Juvenile only.

Phone Queries: N   Unsolicited Mss: N
Mail Queries: Y   Poetry Collections: N
SASE: Y

Curtis Brown, Ltd.
Ten Astor Place
New York, NY 10003
Phone: (212) 473-5400

Contact: Laura Blake Peterson

Agency Commission: not specified

Categories Represented: General trade fiction and
nonfiction, juvenile.

Phone Queries: N   Unsolicited Mss: N
Mail Queries: Y   Poetry Collections: N
SASE: Y

Comments: "Always query first."

Sheree Bykofsky Associates, Inc.
11 East 47th Street
New York, NY 10017
Phone: (212) 308-1253

Contact: Sheree Bykofsky

Agency Commission: not specified

Categories Represented: Adult nonfiction, literary and commercial fiction.

Phone Queries: N   Unsolicited Mss: N
Mail Queries: Y   Poetry Collections: N
SASE: Y

Maria Carvainis Agency, Inc.
235 West End Avenue
New York, NY 10023
Phone: (212) 580-1559

Contact: Maria Carvainis

Agency Commission: 15%   Abroad: 20%

Categories Represented: Fiction: literary and mainstream, contemporary women's, mystery, suspense, fantasy, historical, children's and young adult novels. Nonfiction: business, finance, women's issues, political and film biography, medicine, psychology, and popular science. No film scripts or science fiction.

Phone Queries: N   Unsolicited Mss: N
Mail Queries: Y   Poetry Collections: Y
SASE: Y

Comments: Film scripts are accepted from writers with established credits only. No reading fees.

Martha Casselman, Literary Agent

P.O. Box 342
Calistoga, CA 94515
Phone: (707) 942-4341

Contact: Martha Casselman

Agency Commission: 15%   Abroad: 20%

Categories Represented: Cookbooks and other nonfiction. No fiction or children's.

Phone Queries: Y	Unsolicited Mss: N
Mail Queries: Y	Poetry Collections: N
SASE: Y	

Castiglia Literary Agency

1155 Camino del Mar
Suite 510
Del Mar, CA 92014
Phone: (619) 753-4362   Fax: (619) 753-5094

Contact: Julie Castiglia

Agency Commission: 15%   Abroad: 20%

Categories Represented: Mainstream, literary and ethnic fiction. Nonfiction: psychology, science and health, biography, women's issues, niche books, and contemporary issues.

Phone Queries: N   Unsolicited Mss: N
Mail Queries: Y   Poetry Collections: N
SASE: Y

The Cohen Agency
331 West 57th Street
Suite 176
New York, NY 10019
Phone: (212) 399-9079

Contact: Rob Cohen

Agency Commission: 15%   Abroad: 20%

Categories Represented: Most genre fiction, commercial nonfiction, specializing in women's fiction. No juvenile fiction or short fiction.

Phone Queries: N   Unsolicited Mss: N
Mail Queries: Y   Poetry Collections: N
SASE: Y

Ruth Cohen, Inc.
P.O. Box 7626
Menlo Park, CA 94025
Phone: (415) 854-2054

Contact: Ruth Cohen

Agency Commission: 15%   Abroad: 20%

Categories Represented: Quality women's fiction with unique settings, characters, and plots. Mystery fiction, and well devised, plotted, and characterized juvenile fiction. No screenplays, short stories, poetry, self-help, Westerns, or science fiction.

Phone Queries: Y   Unsolicited Mss: N
Mail Queries: Y   Poetry Collections: N
SASE: Y

Comments: Mail queries must include ten opening manuscript pages and an SASE.

Frances Collin, Literary Agent
P.O. Box 33
Wayne, PA 19087-0033
Phone: (610) 254-0555

Contact: Fran Collin, Marsha Kear

Agency Commission: 15%   Abroad: 20%

Categories Represented: History, biography, some science. Fiction, including fantasy, science fiction, and mysteries. No mathematics, cookbooks, self-help, or New Age.

Phone Queries: N   Unsolicited Mss: N
Mail Queries: Y   Poetry Collections: N
SASE: Y

No reading fees.

Don Congdon Associates, Inc.

156 Fifth Avenue
Suite 625
New York, NY 10010-7002
Phone: (212) 645-1229   Fax: (212) 727-2688
E-mail: doncongdon@aol.com

Contact: Don Congdon, Michael Congdon, Susan
Ramer

Agency Commission: 10%   Abroad: 19%

Categories Represented: Fiction and nonfiction, general trade books for adult audience. No romance.

Phone Queries: N   Unsolicited Mss: N
Mail Queries: Y   Poetry Collections: N
SASE: Y

Comments: Include brief writing sample with mail
queries. No reading fee.

Richard Curtis Associates, Inc.

171 East 74th Street
New York, NY 10021
Phone: (212) 772-7363   Fax: (212) 772-7393

Contact: Richard Curtis, Laura Tucker, Amy Victoria Meo

Agency Commission: 15%   Abroad: 20%

Categories Represented: Quality fiction and nonfiction, health, spiritual, ethnic fiction, multimedia projects, science fiction, romance.

Phone Queries: N   Unsolicited Mss: N
Mail Queries: Y   Poetry Collections: N
SASE: Y

DH Literary, Inc.
P.O. Box 990
Nyack, NY 10160
Phone: (212) 753-7942
E-mail: dhendin@aol.com

Contact: David Hendin

Agency Commission: 15%   Abroad: 20%

Categories Represented: Trade fiction and nonfiction, literary fiction, newspaper syndication, and mysteries. No category fiction, juvenile, or children's.

Phone Queries: N   Unsolicited Mss: N
Mail Queries: Y   Poetry Collections: N
SASE: Y

Darhansoff & Verrill
179 Franklin Street
4th floor
New York, NY 10013
Phone: (212) 334-5980

Contact: Tal Gregory

Agency Commission: 15%   Abroad: 20%/15% for
film

Categories Represented: Literary fiction, serious non-fiction.

Phone Queries: N   Unsolicited Mss: N
Mail Queries: Y   Poetry Collections: N
SASE: Y

Joan Daves Agency/Writers House
21 West 26th Street
New York, NY 10010
Phone: (212) 685-2663   Fax: (212) 685-1781

Contact: Jennifer Lyons

Agency Commission: 15%   Abroad: 20%

Categories Represented: Fiction and nonfiction,
juveniles.

Phone Queries: N   Unsolicited Mss: N
Mail Queries: Y   Poetry Collections: N
SASE: Y

Comments: Mail queries accepted with background information on published work.

Anita Diamant Literary Agency/Writers' Workshop

310 Madison Avenue
New York, NY 10017
Phone: (212) 687-1122   Fax: (212) 687-1756

Contact: Robin Rue, John Talbot, Mark Chelius

Agency Commission: not specified

Categories Represented: Anything but screenplays, children's, science fiction, fantasy, poetry, or short stories.

Phone Queries: N   Unsolicited Mss: N
Mail Queries: Y   Poetry Collections: N
SASE: Y

Sandra Dijkstra Literary Agency

1155 Camino del Mar
Suite 515
Del Mar, CA 92014
Phone: (619) 755-3115   Fax: (619) 792-1494

Contact: Rebecca Lowen

Agency Commission: 15%   Abroad: 20%

Categories Represented: Fiction: specialize in contemporary, literary, mystery/thriller, mainstream, science fiction/fantasy, historical romance. Nonfiction: science, health, history, biography, psychology and self-help, memoir, current affairs, business, and true crime.

Phone Queries: N   Unsolicited Mss: Y
Mail Queries: Y   Poetry Collections: N
SASE: Y

Jonathan Dolger Agency
49 East 96th Street
Suite 9B
New York, NY 10128
Phone: (212) 427-1853   Fax: (212) 369-7118

Contact: Tom Wilson

Agency Commission: 15%   Abroad: 10-15%

Categories Represented: Adult trade fiction and nonfiction. No romance, Westerns, science fiction, or children's.

Phone Queries: N   Unsolicited Mss: N
Mail Queries: Y   Poetry Collections: N
SASE: Y

Donadio & Ashworth, Inc.
121 West 27th Street
Suite 704
New York, NY 10001
Phone: (212) 691-8077   Fax: (212) 633-2837

Contact: Neil Olson, Edward Hibbert, Peter Steinberg

Agency Commission: 15%   Abroad: 20%

Categories Represented: General fiction, nonfiction, and literary fiction. No romance, mystery, or self-help.

Phone Queries: N   Unsolicited Mss: N
Mail Queries: Y   Poetry Collections: N
SASE: Y

Jane Dystel Literary Management
One Union Square West
Suite 904
New York, NY 10003
Phone: (212) 627-9100   Fax: (212) 627-9313
E-mail: jane@dystel.com
or miriam@dystel.com

Contact: Jane Dystel, Miriam Goderich, Eliza Scott, Seanna Beck

Agency Commission: 15%   Abroad: 19%

Categories Represented: General fiction and nonfiction, cookbooks, self-help, science fiction, literary fiction, and New Age. No children's or youth titles, poetry, dramas, or screenplays.

Phone Queries: N   Unsolicited Mss: N
Mail Queries: Y   Poetry Collections: N
SASE: Y

Ann Elmo Agency, Inc.
60 East 42nd Street
New York, NY 10165
Phone: (212) 661-2880   Fax: (212) 661-2883

Contact: Lettie Lee, Andree Abecassis, Mari Cronin

Agency Commission: 15%   Abroad: 20%

Categories Represented: Fiction, nonfiction, and some juvenile.

Phone Queries: Y   Unsolicited Mss: N
Mail Queries: Y   Poetry Collections: N
SASE: Y

Felicia Eth Literary Representation
555 Bryant Street
Suite 350
Palo Alto, CA 94301
Phone: (415) 375-1276   Fax: (415) 375-1277

Contact: Felica Eth

Agency Commission: 15%   Abroad: 20%

Categories Represented: Provocative nonfiction across a variety of categories, journalism, social issues, women's issues, and psychology. High quality mainstream fiction, preferably contemporary. Quirky books accepted occasionally.

Phone Queries: Y   Unsolicited Mss: N
Mail Queries: Y   Poetry Collections: N
SASE: Y

Mary Evans, Inc.
242 East Fifth Street
New York, NY 10003
Phone: (212) 979-0880   Fax: (212) 979-5344
E-mail: merrylit@aol.com

Contact: Mary Evans, Laura Albritton

Agency Commission: 15%   Abroad: 20%

Categories Represented: Literary fiction and nonfiction. No juvenile, romance, science fiction, or Westerns.

Phone Queries: Y   Unsolicited Mss: N
Mail Queries: Y   Poetry Collections: N
SASE: Y

The Fogelman Literary Agency

7515 Greenville Avenue
Suite 712
Dallas, TX 75231
Phone: (214) 361-9956

Contact: Evan M. Fogelman, Linda D. Kruger, Jeannie Maxfield

Agency Commission: 10%   Abroad: 10%

Categories Represented: Women's fiction and nonfiction, including self-help, popular business, and pop culture.

Phone Queries: Y   Unsolicited Mss: N
Mail Queries: Y   Poetry Collections: N
SASE: Y

A Franc Group

2745 Jefferson
Suite B
Carlsbad, CA 92008-1742
Phone: (760) 720-2268   Fax: (760) 720-3763
E-mail: anti@sprynet.com

Contact: Paul Franc

Agency Commission: 10%   Abroad: 10-15%

Categories Represented: Fiction: mystery (no excessive violence or gore) and humor. Nonfiction: computer and electronics, business marketing, and how-to.

Phone Queries: Y	Unsolicited Mss: Y
Mail Queries: Y	Poetry Collections: N
SASE: Y	

Comments: "We are looking for quality feature-length film scripts (no "R"), TV comedies, and original screenplays."

Sarah Jane Freyman Literary Agency

59 West 71st Street
New York, NY 10023
Phone: (212) 362-9277   Fax: (212) 501-8240

Contact: Sarah Jane Freyman

Agency Commission: 15%   Abroad: 20%

Categories Represented: Adult fiction and nonfiction. No category fiction, children's, or poetry.

Phone Queries: N	Unsolicited Mss: Y
Mail Queries: Y	Poetry Collections: N
SASE: Y	

Gelfman Schneider Literary Agents

250 West 57th Street
New York, NY 10107
Phone: (212) 245-1993   Fax: (212) 245-8678
E-mail: gsla@msn.com

Contact: Jane Gelfman, Deborah Schneider

Agency Commission: 15%   Abroad: 20%

Categories Represented: Literary and commercial fiction, nonfiction. No children's or poetry.

Phone Queries: N   Unsolicited Mss: N
Mail Queries: Y   Poetry Collections: N
SASE: Y

Goodman Associates Literary Agents
500 West End Avenue
New York, NY 10024
Phone: (212) 873-4806   Fax: (212) 580-3278

Contact: Arnold P. Goodman, Elise S. Goodman

Agency Commission: 15%   Abroad: 20%

Categories Represented: General adult trade fiction and nonfiction. No poetry, short stories and/or articles, science fiction, or fantasy.

Phone Queries: N   Unsolicited Mss: N
Mail Queries: Y   Poetry Collections: N
SASE: Y

Ashley Grayson Literary Agency
1342 18th Street
San Pedro, CA 90732
Phone: (310) 548-4672   Fax: (310) 514-1148

Contact: Mr. Ashley Grayson

Agency Commission: 15%   Abroad: 20%

Categories Represented: Literary and commercial fiction, some nonfiction, children's, and young adult. No
poetry or screenplays.

Phone Queries: N   Unsolicited Mss: N
Mail Queries: Y   Poetry Collections: N
SASE: Y

Sanford J. Greenburger Associates, Inc.
55 Fifth Avenue
New York, NY 10003
Phone: (212) 206-5600   Fax: (212) 463-8718

Contact: Heide Lange, Faith Hamlin, Beth Vesel,
Theresa Park, Elyse Cheney, Dan Mandel

Agency Commission: 15%   Abroad: 20%

Categories Represented: Fiction and nonfiction.

Phone Queries: N   Unsolicited Mss: N
Mail Queries: Y   Poetry Collections: N
SASE: Y

Maxine Groffsky Literary Agency
853 Broadway
Suite 708
New York, NY 10003
Phone: (212) 979-1500   Fax: (212) 979-1405
E-mail: mgroffsky@aol.com

Contact: Maxine Groffsky

Agency Commission: 15%   Abroad: 20%

Categories Represented: Literary fiction, biography, and memoir.

Phone Queries: N   Unsolicited Mss: N
Mail Queries: Y   Poetry Collections: N
SASE: Y

John Hawkins & Associates, Inc.
71 West 23rd Street
Suite 1600
New York, NY 10010
Phone: (212) 807-7040   Fax: (212) 807-9555

Contact: John Hawkins, William Reiss, Elly Sidel, J. Warren Frazier, Moses Cardona, Luis A. Rios

Agency Commission: 15%   Abroad: 20%

Categories Represented: All fiction and nonfiction. No poetry, screenplays, or plays.

Phone Queries: N
Mail Queries: Y
SASE: Y

Unsolicited Mss: N
Poetry Collections: N

Comments: Accepts mail queries with a cover letter, thirty page sample (first three chapters), include phone number.

Heacock Literary Agency, Inc.
1523 Sixth Street
Suite 14
Santa Monica, CA 90401-2514

Phone: (310) 393-6227

Contact: Rosalie Heacock

Agency Commission: 15%   Abroad: 15-25%

Categories Represented: Good books, nonfiction and fiction. No horror, true crime, or books that are destructive in nature.

Phone Queries: N
Mail Queries: Y
SASE: Y

Unsolicited Mss: N
Poetry Collections: Y

Comments: "Looking for books that make a contribution to society."

Richard Henshaw Group

264 West 73rd Street
New York, NY 10023
Phone: (212) 721-4721   Fax: (212) 721-4208
E-mail: rhgagents@aol.com

Contact: Richard Henshaw

Agency Commission: 15%   Abroad: 20%

Categories Represented: Fiction: literary, thriller, mystery, science fiction, fantasy, horror, young adult. Nonfiction: commercial. No scholarly fiction, story collections, or poetry.

Phone Queries: N   Unsolicited Mss: N
Mail Queries: Y   Poetry Collections: N
SASE: Y

Comments: Accepts proposals (up to fifty pages), fiction or nonfiction.

The Jeff Herman Agency, Inc.

140 Charles Street
Suite 15A
New York, NY 10014
Phone: (212) 941-0540

Contact: Jeff Herman, Deborah Levine, Jamie Forbes

Agency Commission: 15%   Abroad: 10%

Categories Represented: Business, self-help/how-to, computers, history, politics, pop culture, and psychology.

Phone Queries: N   Unsolicited Mss: N
Mail Queries: Y   Poetry Collections: N
SASE: Y

Barbara Hogenson Agency
19 West 44th Street
Suite 1000
New York, NY 10036
Phone: (212) 730-7306   Fax: (212) 730-8970

Contact: Barbara Hogenson, Sarah Felder

Agency Commission: 15%   Abroad: 20%

Categories Represented: Fiction, nonfiction, screenplays, plays, television scripts.

Phone Queries: N   Unsolicited Mss: N
Mail Queries: Y   Poetry Collections: N
SASE: Y

Comments: Also represents stage directors.

International Creative Management, Inc.
40 West 57th Street
New York, NY 10033
Phone: (212) 556-5600

Contact: Amanda Urban, Esther Newberg, Suzanne Gluck, Kristine Dahl, Lisa Bankoff, Mitch Douglas.

Agency Commission: 10%   Abroad: 15-20%

Categories Represented: General fiction and nonfiction, trade adult.

Phone Queries: N   Unsolicited Mss: N
Mail Queries: Y   Poetry Collections: N
SASE: Y

JCA Literary Agency
27 West 20th Street
Suite 1103
New York, NY 10011
Phone: (212) 807-0888

Contact: Jane Cushman, Jeff Gerecke, Tony Outhwaite

Agency Commission: 15%   Abroad: 20%

Categories Represented: Literary and high-grade commercial fiction, mainstream nonfiction, mostly biography, history, current affairs, politics, and the environment. No juvenile books, science fiction, fantasy, how-to, self-help, screenplays, or romances.

Phone Queries: N   Unsolicited Mss: N
Mail Queries: Y   Poetry Collections: N
SASE: Y

Comments: Please send all queries by mail only with SASE.

Sharon Jarvis & Co. (Toad Hall, Inc.)

RR 2, Box 16B
Laceyville, PA 18623
Phone: (717) 869-2942   Fax: (717) 869-1031
E-mail: toadhalco@aol.com

Contact: Sharon Jarvis

Agency Commission: 15%   Abroad: 10%

Categories Represented: Nonfiction, book length only. Fiction only by invitation from previously published writers. No short stories, poetry, scripts, or plays.

Phone Queries: N   Unsolicited Mss: N
Mail Queries: Y   Poetry Collections: N
SASE: Y

Comments: Queries should include total word count, c.v., and SASE. For nonfiction, include detailed table of contents.

Kidde, Hoyt & Picard

335 East 51st Street
New York, NY 10022
Phone: (212) 755-9461   Fax: (212) 223-2501

Contact: Kay Kidde, Laura Langlie

Agency Commission: 15%   Abroad: 7.5%/affiliate
                                            7.5%

Categories Represented: Mainstream literary fiction, romantic fiction, general trade nonfiction. No technical or scholarly, science fiction, male adventure, or juvenile.

Phone Queries: Y   Unsolicited Mss: N
Mail Queries: Y   Poetry Collections: N
SASE: Y

Kirchoff/Wohlberg
202 East 21st Street
Suite 1B
New York, NY 10017

Contact: Sheila Pitchenik

Agency Commission: 15-25%

Categories Represented: Children's material only.

Phone Queries: N   Unsolicited Mss: N
Mail Queries: Y   Poetry Collections: Y
SASE: Y

Kirkland Literary Agency, Inc.
P.O. Box 50608
Amarillo, TX 79159-0608
Phone: (806) 356-0216   Fax: (806) 356-0452

Contact: Jean Price

Agency Commission: 15%   Abroad: 20%

Categories Represented: Specialize in romance. Mainstream mystery, science fiction, fantasy, thriller (extremely selective with horror and Westerns). Non-fiction, on a limited basis. No short stories, poetry, screenplays, magazine articles, or children's.

Phone Queries: Y   Unsolicited Mss: N
Mail Queries: Y   Poetry Collections: N
SASE: Y

Comments: Unsolicited proposals are accepted.

Harvey Klinger
301 West 53rd Street
New York, NY 10019

Phone: (212) 581-7068

Contact: Harvey Klinger

Agency Commission: 15%   Abroad: 25%

Categories Represented: Fiction: literary and commercial. Nonfiction: psychology, health, biography, true crime, popular culture, and how-to.

Phone Queries: N   Unsolicited Mss: N
Mail Queries: Y   Poetry Collections: N
SASE: Y

Barbara S. Kouts, Literary Agent

P.O. Box 560
Bellport, NY 11713
Phone: (516) 286-1278   Fax: (516) 286-1538

Contact: Barbara S. Kouts

Agency Commission: 10%   Abroad: 20%

Categories Represented: Children's fiction and non-fiction, adult fiction, and nonfiction. No romance, science fiction, or Westerns.

Phone Queries: N   Unsolicited Mss: N
Mail Queries: Y   Poetry Collections: N
SASE: Y

Stuart Krichevsky Literary Agency, Inc.

381 Park Avenue South
Suite 819
New York, NY 10016
Phone: (212) 725-5288   Fax: (212) 725-5275

Contact: Stuart Krichevsky

Agency Commission: 15%   Abroad: 20%

Categories Represented: Mystery and suspense, literary fiction, science and technology, narrative nonfiction, journalism, and biography.

Phone Queries: N   Unsolicited Mss: N
Mail Queries: Y   Poetry Collections: N
SASE: Y

The Lantz Office
888 Seventh Avenue
Suite 2500
New York, NY 10106
Phone: (212) 586-0200   Fax: (212) 262-6659

Contact: Robert Lantz, Dennis Aspland

Agency Commission: 10%   Abroad: 20%

Categories Represented: Fiction, nonfiction, and plays.

Phone Queries: N   Unsolicited Mss: N
Mail Queries: Y   Poetry Collections: N
SASE: Y

The Robert Lantz–Joy Harris Literary Agency
136 Fifth Avenue
Suite 617
New York, NY 10010
Phone: (212) 924-6269   Fax: (212) 924-6609

Agency Commission: 15%   Abroad: 20%

Categories Represented: Fiction and nonfiction. No genre fiction, science fiction, or romance.

Phone Queries: N   Unsolicited Mss: N
Mail Queries: Y   Poetry Collections: N
SASE: Y

Michael Larsen/Elizabeth Pomada
Literary Agents
1029 Jones Street
San Francisco, CA 94109
Phone: (415) 673-0939

Contact: Elizabeth Pomada

Agency Commission: 15%   Abroad: 20%

Categories Represented: Commercial, literary, and genre nonfiction for adults. No Westerns, poetry, screenplays, or plays.

Phone Queries: Y   Unsolicited Mss: N
Mail Queries: Y   Poetry Collections: N
SASE: Y

Comments: "We like fresh voices with new ideas."

Lescher & Lescher, Ltd.
67 Irving Place
New York, NY 10003
Phone: (212) 529-1790   Fax: (212) 529-2716

Contact: Robert Lescher, Susan Lescher, Michael Choate

Agency Commission: 15%

Categories Represented: No poetry or screenplays.

Phone Queries: Y   Unsolicited Mss: Y
Mail Queries: Y   Poetry Collections: N
SASE: Y

Levant & Wales Literary Agency, Inc.
108 Hayes Street
Seattle, WA 98109-2808
Phone: (206) 284-7114   Fax: (206) 284-0190

E-mail: bizziew@aol.com

Contact: Elizabeth Wales, Adrienne Reed

Agency Commission: 15%   Abroad: 20%

Categories Represented: Quality fiction and nonfiction. Special interest in "Pacific Rim," West, West Coast, and Northwest writers.

Phone Queries: Y   Unsolicited Mss: N
Mail Queries: Y   Poetry Collections: N
SASE: Y

Ellen Levine Literary Agency

15 East 26th Street
New York, NY 10010
Phone: (212) 889-0620   Fax: (212) 725-4501

Contact: Elizabeth Kaplan

Agency Commission: 15%   Abroad: 20%

Categories Represented: Adult trade nonfiction and fiction. No genre works.

Phone Queries: N   Unsolicited Mss: N
Mail Queries: Y   Poetry Collections: N
SASE: Y

Lichtman, Trister, Singer & Ross

1666 Connecticut Avenue, N.W.
Suite 500
Washington, DC 20009
Phone: (202) 328-1666

Contact: Gail Ross, Howard Yee

Agency Commission: 15%   Abroad: 25%

Categories Represented: Adult commercial fiction and nonfiction.

Phone Queries: N   Unsolicited Mss: N
Mail Queries: Y   Poetry Collections: N
SASE: Y

Nancy Love Literary Agency

250 East 65th Street
Suite 4A
New York, NY 10021
Phone: (212) 980-3499 Fax: (212) 308-6405

Contact: Sherrie Sutton

Agency Commission: 15% Abroad: 20%

Categories Represented: Fiction: mysteries and thrillers. Nonfiction: memoir, biography, self-help, health, alternative health, parenting, inspirational, pop culture, relationships, psychology, nature. No other fiction, children's, young adult, academic, or poetry.

Phone Queries: Y   Unsolicited Mss: N
Mail Queries: Y   Poetry Collections: N
SASE: Y

Lowenstein Associates, Inc.

121 West 27th Street
Suite 601
New York, NY 10001
Phone: (212) 206-1630 Fax: (212) 727-0280

Contact: B. Lowenstein, Nancy Yost

Agency Commission: 15% Abroad: 20%

Categories Represented: Commercial fiction, especially suspense thrillers, mysteries and womens' fiction. Nonfiction: narrative information, self-help, and spirituality. No horror, science fiction, or Westerns.

Phone Queries: N   Unsolicited Mss: N
Mail Queries: Y   Poetry Collections: N
SASE: Y

Donald Maass Literary Agency

157 West 57th Street
Suite 703
New York, NY 10019
Phone: (212) 757-7755

Contact: Donald Maass, Jennifer Jackson

Agency Commission: 15%   Abroad: 20%

Categories Represented: Specialize in fiction: all categories of commercial and literary fiction, with an emphasis on mystery/suspense, science fiction/fantasy, romance/women's. No nonfiction or juvenile fiction.

Phone Queries: N   Unsolicited Mss: N
Mail Queries: Y   Poetry Collections: N
SASE: Y

Carol Mann Agency

55 Fifth Avenue
New York, NY 10003

Contact: Carol Mann, Christy Fletcher, Ms. Gareth Esersky

Agency Commission: 15%   Abroad: 20%

Categories Represented: Nonfiction: women's issues, childcare and parenting, politics. Fiction: literary fiction. No genre fiction, romance, historical, science fiction, or mysteries.

Phone Queries: N   Unsolicited Mss: N
Mail Queries: Y   Poetry Collections: N
SASE: Y

Manus and Associates Literary Agency, Inc.
417 East 57th Street
Suite 5D
New York, NY 10022
Phone: (212) 644-8020   Fax: (212) 644-3374

Contact: Janet Wilkens Manus

Agency Commission: 15%   Abroad: 10%

Categories Represented: Specialize in true crime, mysteries, and thrillers. Also commercial fiction. No romance or science fiction.

Phone Queries: N   Unsolicited Mss: N
Mail Queries: Y   Poetry Collections: N
SASE: Y

Comments: West Coast office: 430 Cowper Street, Palo Alto, CA 94301; Phone (415) 617-4556; Contact Jillian Manus.

Denise Marcil Literary Agency, Inc.
685 West End Avenue
Suite 9C
New York, NY 10025
Phone: (212) 932-3110

Contact: Denise Marcil

Agency Commission: 15%   Abroad: 20%

Categories Represented: Commercial women's fiction, romance, mainstream suspense and thrillers. Popular reference including: psychological self-help, parenting, business, health, spirituality, and personal finance.

Phone Queries: N   Unsolicited Mss: N
Mail Queries: Y   Poetry Collections: N
SASE: Y

Mildred Marmur Associates Ltd.
2005 Palmer Avenue
Suite 127
Larchmont, NY 10538
Phone: (914) 834-1170   Fax: (914) 834-2840

Contact: Mildred Marmur, Jane Lebowitz

Agency Commission: 15%   Abroad: 20%

Categories Represented: Serious nonfiction, some juvenile, cookbooks, and literary fiction. No science fiction, poetry, or category fiction.

Phone Queries: N   Unsolicited Mss: N
Mail Queries: Y   Poetry Collections: N
SASE: Y

Margaret McBride Literary Agency
7744 Fay Avenue
Suite 201
La Jolla, CA 92037
Phone: (619) 454-1550   Fax: (619) 454-2156

Contact: Mindy Riesenberg

Agency Commission: 15%   Abroad: 25%

Categories Represented: Mainstream fiction and nonfiction. No romance, mystery, or poetry.

Phone Queries: N   Unsolicited Mss: N
Mail Queries: Y   Poetry Collections: N
SASE: Y

McIntosh and Otis, Inc.
310 Madision Avenue
New York, NY 10017
Phone: (212) 687-7400   Fax: (212) 687-6894

Contact: Eugene Winick, Renee Cho, Dorothy Markinko, Samuel Pinkus, Evva Joan Pryor

Agency Commission: 15%

Categories Represented: Adult and juvenile literary fiction and nonfiction.

Phone Queries: N   Unsolicited Mss: N
Mail Queries: Y   Poetry Collections: N
SASE: Y

Claudia Menza Literary Agency
1170 Broadway
Room 807
New York, NY 10001
Phone: (212) 889-6850

Contact: Claudia Menza, Richard Derus

Agency Commission: 15%   Abroad: 20%

Categories Represented: Idiosyncratic fiction and nonfiction. No romance or poetry.

Phone Queries: N   Unsolicited Mss: N
Mail Queries: Y   Poetry Collections: N
SASE: Y

Helen Merrill, Ltd.
425 West 23rd Street
Suite 1F
New York, NY 10011
Phone: (212) 691-5326   Fax: (212) 727-0545

Contact: Helen Merrill, Patrick Herold

Agency Commission: 10%   Abroad: 10%/20%
                                                              Amateur

Categories Represented: Theatrical, movies, books.
No poetry.

Phone Queries: N   Unsolicited Mss: N
Mail Queries: Y   Poetry Collections: N
SASE: Y

Multimedia Product Development, Inc.
410 South Michigan Avenue
Suite 724
Chicago, IL 60605
Phone: (312) 922-3063   Fax: (312) 922-1905
E-mail: mpdinc@aol.com

Contact: Jane Jordan Browne

Agency Commission: 15%   Abroad: 20%

Categories Represented: Adult fiction and nonfiction
for the commercial market; also juvenile fiction and

nonfiction. No horror, science fiction, short stories, poetry, or original screenplays.

Phone Queries: N	Unsolicited Mss: N
Mail Queries: Y	Poetry Collections: N
SASE: Y	

Comments: E-mail queries not accepted. "We are interested in mainstream, overnight sellers."

Jean V. Naggar Literary Agency

216 East 75th Street
New York, NY 10021
Phone: (212) 794-1082

Contact: Jean Naggar, Frances Kuffel, Anne Engel

Agency Commission: 15%   Abroad: 20%

Categories Represented: High quality mainstream fiction, mystery suspense, literary fiction, and historicals. Nonfiction: biography, women's studies, literary memoirs, science, psychology, and sophisticated self-help, some children's. No romance, category, or formula fiction, science fiction, or sports.

Phone Queries: Y	Unsolicited Mss: N
Mail Queries: Y	Poetry Collections: N
SASE: Y	

New England Publishing Associates, Inc.

P.O. Box 5
Chester, CT 06412
Phone: (860) 345-7323   Fax: (860) 345-3660
E-mail: nepa@nepa.com

Contact: Elizabeth Frost-Knappman

Agency Commission: 15%   Abroad: 20%

Categories Represented: True crime, women's studies, literature, biographies, reference, current events, and history.

Phone Queries: Y   Unsolicited Mss: N
Mail Queries: Y   Poetry Collections: N
SASE: Y

The Betsy Nolan Literary Agency

224 West 29th Street
15th floor
New York, NY 10001
Phone: (212) 967-8200   Fax: (212) 967-7292

Contact: Carla Glasser, Donald Lehr, Ellen Morrissey

Agency Commission: 15%   Abroad: 15%

Categories Represented: Specialize in nonfiction: popular culture and music, gardening, child care, cookbooks, how-to, biography, African-American, and Judaica. Some literary fiction. No poetry.

Phone Queries: N   Unsolicited Mss: N
Mail Queries: Y   Poetry Collections: N
SASE: Y

Harold Ober Associates, Inc.
425 Madison Avenue
New York, NY 10017
Phone: (212) 759-8600   Fax: (212) 759-9428

Agency Commission: 15%   Abroad: 20%

Categories Represented: Fiction and nonfiction, primarily booklength. No poetry, plays, or screenplays.

Phone Queries: N   Unsolicited Mss: N
Mail Queries: Y   Poetry Collections: N
SASE: Y

Alice Orr Agency, Inc.
305 Madison Avenue
Suite 1166
New York, NY 10165
Phone: (718) 204-6673   Fax: (718) 204-6673
E-mail: orragency@aol.com

Contact: Alice Orr

Agency Commission: not specified

Categories Represented: Not accepting new clients as of publication date.

Phone Queries: N	Unsolicited Mss: N
Mail Queries: N	Poetry Collections: N
SASE: N	

Fifi Oscard Agency, Inc.
24 West 40th Street
New York, NY 10018
Phone: (212) 764-1100   Fax: (212) 840-5019

Contact: Literary Department

Agency Commission: 15%   Abroad: 20%

Categories Represented: General nonfiction: biography, celebrity biography, pop culture, and sports. Fiction: literary and mysteries. Some children's.

Phone Queries: N	Unsolicited Mss: N
Mail Queries: Y	Poetry Collections: N
SASE: Y	

The Richard Parks Agency
138 East 16th Street
Suite 5B
New York, NY 10003
Phone: (212) 254-9067

Contact: Richard Parks

Agency Commission: 15%   Abroad: 20%

Categories Represented: Literary and commercial fiction, narrative and general nonfiction. No romance, Westerns, or fantasy.

Phone Queries: N   Unsolicited Mss: N
Mail Queries: Y   Poetry Collections: N
SASE: Y

Pelham-Heuisler Literary Agency
2496 North Palo Santo Drive
Tuscon, AZ 85745
Phone: (520) 624-7741

Contact: Bill Heuisler

Agency Commission: 15%

Categories Represented: Fiction and nonfiction, all categories, all genres. No children's.

Phone Queries: N   Unsolicited Mss: N
Mail Queries: Y   Poetry Collections: N
SASE: Y

James Peter Associates, Inc.
P.O. Box 772
Tenafly, NJ 07670
Phone: (201) 568-0760   Fax: (201) 568-2959

Contact: Bert Holtje

Agency Commission: 15%   Abroad: 20%

Categories Represented: Adult nonfiction—all categories.

Phone Queries: N   Unsolicited Mss: N
Mail Queries: Y   Poetry Collections: N
SASE: Y

Pinder Lane & Garon-Brooke Associates, Ltd.
159 West 53rd Street
Suite 14E
New York, NY 10019
Phone: (212) 489-0880   Fax: (212) 586-9346
E-mail: pinderl@interport.net

Contact: Dick Duane, Robert Thixton

Agency Commission: 15%   Abroad: 30%

Categories Represented: All types of fiction. Nonfiction: lifestyle, popular culture, historical biography, investigative reporting, and natural history.

Phone Queries: Y   Unsolicited Mss: N
Mail Queries: Y   Poetry Collections: N
SASE: Y

Aaron M. Priest Literary Agency, Inc.
708 Third Avenue
23rd floor
New York, NY 10017
Phone: (212) 818-0344   Fax: (212) 573-9417

Contact: Aaron M. Priest, Molly Friedrich, Lisa Erbach Vance

Agency Commission: 15%   Abroad: 10%

Categories Represented: Literary and commercial fiction and nonfiction, thrillers, mystery, and romance.

Phone Queries: N   Unsolicited Mss: N
Mail Queries: Y   Poetry Collections: N
SASE: Y

Susan Ann Protter Literary Agent
110 West 40th Street
Suite 1408
New York, NY 10018
Phone: (212) 840-0480

Contact: Christina Prestia

Agency Commission: 15%   Abroad: 20%

Categories Represented: Thrillers, self-help, parenting, mathematical, science fiction, true crime, mystery. No romance, Westerns, poetry, novellas, scripts, or plays. No *Star Wars*- or *Star Trek*-type science fiction.

Phone Queries: N

Mail Queries: Y

SASE: Y

Unsolicited Mss: N

Poetry Collections: N

Comments: A handling fee of $10 will be required if a manuscript is requested.

Raines & Raines
71 Park Avenue
New York, NY 10016
Phone: (212) 684-5160

Contact: Theron Raines, Joan Raines, Keith Korman

Agency Commission: 15%   Abroad: 20%

Categories Represented: None specified.

Phone Queries: Y

Mail Queries: Y

SASE: Y

Unsolicited Mss: N

Poetry Collections: N

Helen Rees Literary Agency
308 Commonwealth Avenue
Boston, MA 02115
Phone: (617) 262-2401   Fax: (617) 236-0133

Contact: Joan Mazmanian

Agency Commission: 15%   Abroad: 30%

Categories Represented: Business, biography, literary fiction, self-help. No poetry, science fiction, children's, young adult, photography, cookbooks, or short stories.

Phone Queries: N   Unsolicited Mss: N
Mail Queries: Y   Poetry Collections: N
SASE: Y

The Naomi Reichstein Literary Agency

5031 Foothills Road, Room G
Lake Oswego, OR 97034
Phone: (503) 636-7575   Fax: (503) 636-3957
E-mail: nreichstein@northwest.com

Contact: Naomi Wittes Reichstein

Agency Commission: 15%   Abroad: 20%

Categories Represented: Quality adult fiction. Nonfiction including: history, cultural studies and issues, travel, geography, environment, science, music, arts, architecture, memoirs, literature, psychology, how-to, and humor. No science fiction, horror, category romance, children's or young adult, individual articles or short stories, plays, film or television scripts, collections of poetry, or works on the paranormal.

Phone Queries: N   Unsolicited Mss: N
Mail Queries: Y   Poetry Collections: N
SASE: Y

Comments: Queries also accepted by E-mail, but no attachments or manuscripts.

Rights Unlimited

101 West 55th Street
Suite 2D
New York, NY 10019
Phone: (212) 246-0900   Fax: (212) 246-2114

Contact: Bernard Kurman

Agency Commission: 15%   Abroad: 25%

Categories Represented: All categories with the exception of poetry, short stories, plays, movie scripts.

Phone Queries: N   Unsolicited Mss: Y
Mail Queries: Y   Poetry Collections: N
SASE: Y

Ann Rittenberg Literary Agency

14 Montgomery Place
Brooklyn, NY 11215
Phone: (718) 857-1460   Fax: (718) 857-1484

Contact: Ann Rittenberg

Agency Commission: 15%   Abroad: 20%

Categories Represented: Literary fiction. Nonfiction: cultural and social history, biography, gardening, women's issues, memoirs.

Phone Queries: N   Unsolicited Mss: N
Mail Queries: Y   Poetry Collections: N
SASE: Y

Rosenstone/Wender
3 East 48th Street
4th floor
New York, NY 10017

Phone: (212) 832-8330   Fax: (212) 759-4524

Contact: Phyllis Wender, Susan Perlman Cohen, Hannah Wallace

Agency Commission: 15%   Abroad: 20%

Categories Represented: Fiction and nonfiction, film, T.V. rights, children's fiction and nonfiction.

Phone Queries: N   Unsolicited Mss: N
Mail Queries: Y   Poetry Collections: N
SASE: Y

Jane Rotrosen Agency

318 East 51st Street
New York, NY 10022
Phone: (212) 593-4330   Fax: (212) 935-6985

Contact: Ruth Kagle, Stephanie Tape, Meg Ruley, Andrea Cirillo

Agency Commission: 15%   Abroad: 20%

Categories Represented: General fiction and non-fiction.

Phone Queries: Y   Unsolicited Mss: N
Mail Queries: Y   Poetry Collections: N
SASE: Y

Pesha Rubinstein Literary Agency, Inc.

1392 Rugby Road
Teaneck, NJ 07666
Phone: (201) 862-1174   Fax: (201) 862-1180

Contact: Pesha Rubinstein

Agency Commission: 15%   Abroad: 20%

Categories Represented: Literary and commercial adult fiction, middle grade fiction and nonfiction, children's picture books (authors and illustrators). No poetry, Westerns, or men's adventures.

Phone Queries: Y   Unsolicited Mss: N
Mail Queries: Y   Poetry Collections: N
SASE: Y

Comments: Mail queries must include first 10 pages of manuscript and SASE.

Russell & Volkening
50 West 29th Street
Suite 7E
New York, NY 10001
Phone: (212) 684-6050   Fax: (212) 889-3026

Contact: Timothy Seldes, Joseph Regal, Jennie Dunham, Jonathan Delcourt

Agency Commission: 10%   Abroad: 20%

Categories Represented: Literary fiction and nonfiction, juvenile. No horror, science fiction, romance or poetry.

Phone Queries: N   Unsolicited Mss: N
Mail Queries: Y   Poetry Collections: N
SASE: Y

The Sagalyn Agency
4825 Bethesda Avenue
Suite 302
Bethesda, MD 20814
Phone: (301) 718-6440

Agency Commission: not specified

Categories Represented: Adult fiction and nonfiction. No children's, cookbooks, poetry, or young adult.

Phone Queries: N   Unsolicited Mss: N
Mail Queries: Y   Poetry Collections: N
SASE: Y

Victoria Sanders

241 Avenue of the Americas
New York, NY 10014
Phone: (212) 633-8811   Fax: (212) 633-0525

Contact: Victoria Sanders, Diane Dickensheid

Agency Commission: 15%   Abroad: 20%

Categories Represented: Literary and commercial fiction, especially African-American, Latin, and Asian, all nonfiction, especially women's issues, history and politics. No academic or children's.

Phone Queries: N   Unsolicited Mss: N
Mail Queries: Y   Poetry Collections: N
SASE: Y

Comments: Mail queries should include a synopsis or outline.

Harold Schmidt Literary Agency

343 West 12th Street
Suite 1B
New York, NY 10014
Phone: (212) 727-7473   Fax: (212) 807-6025
E-mail: hslanyc@aol.com

Contact: Harold Schmidt

Agency Commission: 15%   Abroad: 20%

Categories Represented: Fiction and nonfiction. No juvenile, romance, or science fiction.

Phone Queries: N   Unsolicited Mss: N
Mail Queries: Y   Poetry Collections: N
SASE: Y

Comments: No reading fees.

Susan Schulman, A Literary Agency

454 West 44th Street
New York, NY 10036
Phone: (212) 713-1633   Fax: (212) 581-8830
E-mail: schulman@aol.com

Contact: Susan Schulman

Agency Commission: 15%   Abroad: 20%

Categories Represented: Specialize in nonfiction of all types: particularly psychology-based self-help for women and families. Also, business, social science, biography, linguistics. Fiction: mysteries, historicals, thrillers. Studies: on creativity, gender and the arts, writing processes.

Phone Queries: N   Unsolicited Mss: N
Mail Queries: Y   Poetry Collections: Y
SASE: Y

Comments: Collections of poetry considered with query including a sample. Poet must be previously published.

Sebastian Literary Agency

333 Kearny Street
Suite 708
San Francisco, CA 94108
Phone: (415) 391-2331
Email: harper@aol.com

Contact: Laurie Harper

Agency Commission: 15%   Abroad: 20-25%

Categories Represented: Specialize in business: career, finance, and investment, consumer reference. Also psychology and self-help.

Phone Queries: N   Unsolicited Mss: N
Mail Queries: Y   Poetry Collections: N
SASE: Y

Rosalie Siegel International
Literary Agent, Inc.

1 Abey Drive
Pennington, NJ 08534
Phone: (609) 737-1007   Fax: (609) 737-3708

Contact: Rosalie Siegel, Antonia Prescott

Agency Commission: 10%   Abroad: 20%

Categories Represented: Adult fiction and nonfiction.

Phone Queries: N   Unsolicited Mss: N
Mail Queries: Y   Poetry Collections: N
SASE: Y

Irene Skolnick Agency

121 West 27th Street
Suite 601
New York, NY 10001
Phone: (212) 727-3698   Fax: (212) 727-1024

Contact: Irene Skolnick

Agency Commission: 15%   Abroad: 20%

Categories Represented: Literary fiction, biography, narrative nonfiction, memoir, travel, and contemporary culture. No screenplays, children's, science fiction, humor, or New Age.

Phone Queries: Y   Unsolicited Mss: N
Mail Queries: Y   Poetry Collections: N
SASE: N

Comments: Mail queries should include sample chapters.

Smith/Skolnick Literary Management
303 Walnut Street
Westfield, NJ 07090
Phone: (908) 654-5758   Fax: (908) 654-5776

Contact: Nikki Smith, Sandy King

Agency Commission: 15%   Abroad: 20%

Categories Represented: Fiction and nonfiction. No science fiction, fantasy, romance, children's, business, or self-help.

Phone Queries: Y   Unsolicited Mss: N
Mail Queries: Y   Poetry Collections: N
SASE: Y

Philip G. Spitzer Literary Agency
50 Talmage Farm Lane
East Hampton, NY 11937
Phone: (516) 329-3650   Fax: (516) 329-3651

Contact: Philip G. Spitzer

Agency Commission: 15%   Abroad: 20%

Categories Represented: Literary fiction, suspense fiction, and general nonfiction. No "how-to."

Phone Queries: N   Unsolicited Mss: N
Mail Queries: Y   Poetry Collections: N
SASE: Y

Gloria Stern Agency
2929 Buffalo Speedway
Suite 2111
Houston, TX 77098
Phone: (713) 963-8360   Fax: (713) 963-8460

Contact: Gloria Stern

Agency Commission: 15%   Abroad: 10%

Categories Represented: Literary and mainstream novels. Nonfiction by experts in their fields: history, biography, science, health, and more. No romance, science fiction, mystery, poetry, or individual short stories.

Phone Queries: Y   Unsolicited Mss: N
Mail Queries: Y   Poetry Collections: N
SASE: Y

Robin Straus Agency, Inc.
229 East 79th Street
New York, NY 10021
Phone: (212) 472-3282

Contact: Robin Straus

Agency Commission: 15%   Abroad: 20%

Categories Represented: High quality adult fiction and nonfiction.

Phone Queries: N   Unsolicited Mss: Y
Mail Queries: Y   Poetry Collections: N
SASE: Y

Comments: Unsolicited, partial manuscripts must weigh less than one pound and include SASE.

Emma Sweeney Literary Agency
245 East 80th Street
New York, NY 10021
Phone: (212) 734-1874

Agency Commission: 15%   Abroad: 10%

Categories Represented: Literary fiction and general nonfiction.

Phone Queries: N   Unsolicited Mss: N
Mail Queries: Y   Poetry Collections: N
SASE: Y

Roslyn Targ Literary Agency, Inc.

105 West 13th Street
New York, NY 10011-7848
Phone: (212) 206-9390   Fax: (212) 989-6233
E-mail: roslyntarg@aol.com

Contact: Roslyn Targ

Agency Commission: 15%   Abroad: 20%

Categories Represented: First novels: commercial and literary. Nonfiction: general and self-help. No science fiction.

Phone Queries: N   Unsolicited Mss: N
Mail Queries: Y   Poetry Collections: N
SASE: Y

Ralph M. Vicinanza, Ltd.

111 8th Avenue
Suite 1501
New York, NY 10011
Phone: (212) 924-7090   Fax: (212) 691-9644

Contact: Ralph Vicinanza, Chris Lotts, Sharon Friedman

Agency Commission: not specified

Categories Represented: Fiction: literary, women's, multicultural, and popular (especially science fiction, fantasy, and thrillers). Nonfiction: history, business, science, biography, popular culture, and children's. Foreign rights specialists.

Phone Queries: N   Unsolicited Mss: N
Mail Queries: Y   Poetry Collections: N
SASE: Y

Mary Jack Wald Associates, Inc.

111 East 14th Street
New York, NY 10003
Phone: (212) 254-7842

Contact: Davis Sher

Agency Commission: 15%   Abroad: 15%

Categories Represented: Fiction and nonfiction, adult and juvenile. No cookbooks, computer, or textbooks.

Phone Queries: N   Unsolicited Mss: N
Mail Queries: Y   Poetry Collections: N
SASE: Y

The Wallace Literary Agency

177 East 70th Street
New York, NY 10021
Phone: (212) 540-9090   Fax: (212) 772-8979

Contact: Tom Wallace

Agency Commission: 15%   Abroad: 20%

Categories Represented: Serious fiction. Nonfiction: history, biography, memoir, belles-lettres, criticism, investigative journalism.

Phone Queries: N
Mail Queries: Y
SASE: Y

Unsolicited Mss: N
Poetry Collections: N

Harriet Wasserman Literary Agency, Inc.
137 East 36th Street
New York, NY 10016
Phone: (212) 689-3257

Contact: Harriet Wasserman

Agency Commission: 10%   Abroad: 20%

Categories Represented: High quality literary fiction and nonfiction.

Phone Queries: N
Mail Queries: N
SASE: N

Unsolicited Mss: N
Poetry Collections: N

Comments: By referral only.

The Wendy Weil Agency, Inc.
232 Madison Avenue
Suite 1300
New York, NY 10016
Phone: (212) 685-0030   Fax: (212) 685-0795

Contact: Wendy Weil

Agency Commission: 15%   Abroad: 20%

Categories Represented: Fiction and nonfiction. No screenplays, children's literature, or poetry.

Phone Queries: N   Unsolicited Mss: N
Mail Queries: Y   Poetry Collections: N
SASE: Y

Rhoda Weyr Agency
151 Bergen Street
Brooklyn, NY 11217
Phone: (718) 522-0480   Fax: (718) 522-0410

Contact: Rhoda Weyr

Agency Commission: not specified

Categories Represented: Nonfiction and fiction. No science fiction, romance, poetry, or cookbooks.

Phone Queries: N   Unsolicited Mss: Y
Mail Queries: Y   Poetry Collections: N
SASE: Y

Comments: Unsolicited manuscripts must include SASE.

WordMaster

4317 West Farrand Road
Clio, MI 48420
Phone: (810) 687-7792

Contact: Judith Karns

Agency Commission: 15%   Abroad: 20%

Categories Represented: All fiction. Nonfiction with appropriate credentials. No sexual content.

Phone Queries: N   Unsolicited Mss: N
Mail Queries: Y   Poetry Collections: N
SASE: Y

Comments: Mail queries must include a three page proposal and three chapters, with SASE.

Writers House, Inc.

21 West 26th Street
New York, NY 10010
Phone: (212) 685-2400   Fax: (212) 685-1781

Contact: Albert Zuckerman

Agency Commission: 10% juvenile, 15% adult
Abroad: 20%

Categories Represented: Fiction: suspense novels, fantasy, science fiction, popular nonfiction, juvenile and young adult series. No poetry, film, television, or stage scripts, short stories, or magazine articles.

Phone Queries: N   Unsolicited Mss: N
Mail Queries: Y   Poetry Collections: N
SASE: Y

Mary Yost Associates, Inc.
59 East 54th Street
New York, NY 10022
Phone: (212) 980-4988   Fax: (212) 935-3632

Contact: Mary Yost

Agency Commission: 15%   Abroad: 10%

Categories Represented: General fiction and nonfiction. Specialize in psychology, spiritual, New Age, women's studies, and biography.

Phone Queries: Y   Unsolicited Mss: N
Mail Queries: Y   Poetry Collections: N
SASE: Y

Susan Zeckendorf Associates, Inc.
171 West 57th Street
New York, NY 10019
Phone: (212) 245-2928

Contact: Susan Zeckendorf

Agency Commission: 15%   Abroad: 20%

Categories Represented: Literary fiction, women's commercial fiction, mystery, thrillers. Nonfiction: science, self-help, social history, biography, music. No science fiction, romance, or business.

Phone Queries: Y   Unsolicited Mss: N
Mail Queries: Y   Poetry Collections: N
SASE: Y

WHERE TO FIND MORE AGENTS

BOOKS

The reference books listed below can be found in most libraries.

A Guide to Literary Agents
Writer's Digest Books
1507 Dana Avenue
Cincinnati, OH 45207
Phone: (800) 289-0963 outside Ohio; (513) 531-2222 in Ohio

Annual. $21.99

The 1996 edition lists 475 agencies, both commission and fee-charging.

Information given: name of agency; address; principal contact; commission rate: kinds of work handled. Further information may include: policy on unsolicited queries and manuscripts; tips on submitting work to agents and editors; recent sales.

The Insider's Guide to Book Editors, Publishers and Literary Agents
Jeff Herman
Prima Communications
Box 1260
Rocklin, CA 95677-1260
Phone: (916) 632-4400

Annual. 1996–97 edition $22.95

Select listing of agents, approximately 100, who responded to a survey Herman devised. All are members of AAR. Includes idiosyncratic information such as what the agent will and will not represent, when and where they were born and educated, their career history, and their agenting track record.

Literary Market Place (LMP)

R.R. Bowker Company
245 West 17th Street
New York, NY 10011
Orders: (800) 521-8110

Annual. $189.99

LMP is the "phone book" of the trade publishing industry.
It includes a comprehensive listing of book agents: all
reputable commission agents and some "mixed" agencies (commission and fee-charging). To be listed,
agencies must provide letters of reference from publishers that show the agents to be well established and
active in the previous year.

The 1996 edition lists more than 500 literary and dramatic agents.

Information given: name of agency; address; telephone
number; principal contact. Further information may
include: names of all agents in the firm; names of
foreign representatives; specific areas of interest; policies on manuscript submission; membership listing.

ORGANIZATIONS

Association of Authors' Representatives (AAR)
10 Astor Place, 3rd floor
New York, NY 10003.
Phone: (212) 353-3709

A nonprofit membership organization of approximately 250 literary and dramatic agents, the AAR was formed in 1991 through the merger of the Society of Authors' Representatives (founded in 1928) and the Independent Literary Agents Association (founded in 1977). At regular meetings and seminars, AAR members discuss important issues concerning writers and agents. The AAR aims to keep agents informed about conditions in publishing, the theater, the motion picture and television industries, and related fields; encourage cooperation among literary organizations; and assist agents in representing their author-clients' interests.

For $7.00 (check or money order) plus a #10 self-addressed envelope stamped with 55¢ postage, the AAR provides a brochure that outlines its objectives and describes the author-agent relationship; a listing of its members with their addresses and phone numbers; and a copy of its Canon of Ethics.

To qualify for membership, an agent must meet professional standards specified by the organization's bylaws and agree to subscribe to its Canon of Ethics.

The AAR will accept no agents who charge reading fees.

International Women's Writing Guild
P.O. Box 810
Gracie Station
New York, NY 10016
Phone: (212) 737-7536

Provides an agent list to members and holds "Meet the Agents and Editors" in April and October.

Society of Children's Book Writers & Illustrators
22736 Van Owen Street, #106
West Hills, CA 91307

Provides a list of agents to its members.

Writers Guild of America, East, Inc.
555 West 57th Street
Suite 1230
New York, NY 10019
Phone: (212) 767-7800
Fax: (212) 582-1909
or
Writers Guild of America, West, Inc.
7000 West 3rd Street
Los Angeles, CA 90048
Phone: (213) 951-4000
Fax: (213) 782-4800

List of screenplay agents:

WGA, East—$1.08 at the Guild office, $1.40 if mailed in New York State, and $1.32 if mailed out of state. Check or money order only.

WGA, West—free at the Guild office; $2 and SASE if mailed.

A comprehensive and reliable list for those who write for radio, television, and film. All agencies on the list have signed the Guild's Artists-Manager Basic Agreement (AMBA). All agree to charge no fee other than a 10% commission on sales.

Information given: name of agency; address; telephone number; whether or not agency handles "material from novice writers."

MORE RESOURCES FROM POETS & WRITERS, INC.

Poets & Writers Magazine. "A storehouse of information about grants, awards, fellowships, workshops, publications, and other inside business, as well as a serious magazine about the writing life."—*Chicago Sun-Times.* Bimonthly. Sample issue, $3.95.
One year subscription, $19.95.   ISSN 089161136

A Directory of American Poets and Fiction Writers. 1997–98 Edition. Over 7,000 writers—names, addresses, phone numbers, E-mail and Web addresses, and recent publications.
344 pages. $27.95.   ISBN 0-913734-58-6

Into Print: Guides to the Writing Life. The best practical articles from *Poets & Writers Magazine.* Find out: How to

publish your manuscript . . . how much your book is worth . . . and much more!
212 pages. $12.95.   ISBN 0-913734-48-9

A Writer's Guide to Copyright. Second Edition. Everything you need to copyright your work, plus sample forms, a standard book contract, and two Copyright Office registration forms.
63 pages. $6.95.   ISBN 0-913734-21-7

Writers Conferences List. Over 200 listings of conferences and festivals in the United States and abroad: dates, addresses, fees, deadlines, and workshop leaders. Updated annually.
101 pages. $12.   ISBN 0-913734-59-4

Rising Voices: A Guide to Young Writers' Resources, Second Edition. Over 200 resources for young poets, fiction writers, and playwrights, grades K through 12.
48 pages. $8.   ISBN 0-913734-60-8

Poets & Writers welcomes orders from individuals who may not have access to bookstores that carry our publications. Please add $3.90 for shipping and handling. Call, write, or E-mail to request a complete catalogue.

Poets & Writers, Inc.
72 Spring Street
New York, NY 10012
Phone: (212) 226-3586
Fax: (212) 226-3963
E-mail: PWSubs@pw.org
Visit our Web site: http://www.pw.org

ABOUT POETS & WRITERS

Since 1970 Poets & Writers, Inc., a nonprofit organization, has been the central source of practical information for the literary community in the United States. Poets and fiction writers are solitary workers, and the services of Poets & Writers fill their need for community, communication, and professional information.

Information Services offers additional resources to writers, including information on publishing opportunities and literary agents. In New York City, we also host publishing seminars to help writers understand the literary marketplace. If you would like a free packet or seminars brochure (specify), simply write to Information Services, Poets & Writers, Inc., 72 Spring Street, New York, NY 10012, or call 212-226-3586, check out our Web page at http://www.pw.org, or E-mail us at infocenter@pw.org.

Our **Readings/Workshops Program,** active in New York State, California, Detroit, and Chicago, provides matching fees for readings and workshops given by emerging and established writers in diverse urban and rural settings. **The Writers Exchange** is a national program that introduces emerging writers to literary communities outside their home states. To date, over forty writers from seventeen states have participated. **Writers on Site** offers multi-disciplinary residencies for writers working in partnership with visual and literary arts organizations in California. For more information on any of these programs, call 212-226-3586.

We also cosponsor **The Literary Network,** which encourages writers, editors, publishers, and others to champion freedom of expression and public funding for the arts. For more information, you may call 212-226-3586.

Contributors to Poets & Writers make it possible for us to accomplish our mission. With your support we can assist many more emerging poets and fiction writers. For information on how to make a tax-deductible contribution, please call or write our Development Department.

Poets & Writers is grateful to the National Endowment for the Arts, the New York State Council on the Arts, the New York City Department of Cultural Affairs, and the foundations, corporations, and individuals that have generously supported our programs for more than twenty-five years.

FOR THE BEST IN PAPERBACKS, LOOK FOR THE

In every corner of the world, on every subject under the sun, Penguin represents quality and variety—the very best in publishing today.

For complete information about books available from Penguin—including Puffins, Penguin Classics, and Arkana—and how to order them, write to us at the appropriate address below. Please note that for copyright reasons the selection of books varies from country to country.

In the United Kingdom: Please write to *Dept. JC, Penguin Books Ltd, FREEPOST, West Drayton, Middlesex UB7 0BR*.

If you have any difficulty in obtaining a title, please send your order with the correct money, plus ten percent for postage and packaging, to *P.O. Box No. 11, West Drayton, Middlesex UB7 0BR*

In the United States: Please write to *Consumer Sales, Penguin USA, P.O. Box 999, Dept. 17109, Bergenfield, New Jersey 07621-0120*. VISA and MasterCard holders call 1-800-253-6476 to order all Penguin titles

In Canada: Please write to *Penguin Books Canada Ltd, 10 Alcorn Avenue, Suite 300, Toronto, Ontario M4V 3B2*

In Australia: Please write to *Penguin Books Australia Ltd, P.O. Box 257, Ringwood, Victoria 3134*

In New Zealand: Please write to *Penguin Books (NZ) Ltd, Private Bag 102902, North Shore Mail Centre, Auckland 10*

In India: Please write to *Penguin Books India Pvt Ltd, 706 Eros Apartments, 56 Nehru Place, New Delhi 110 019*

In the Netherlands: Please write to *Penguin Books Netherlands bv, Postbus 3507, NL-1001 AH Amsterdam*

In Germany: Please write to *Penguin Books Deutschland GmbH, Metzlerstrasse 26, 60594 Frankfurt am Main*

In Spain: Please write to *Penguin Books S. A., Bravo Murillo 19, 1° B, 28015 Madrid*

In Italy: Please write to *Penguin Italia s.r.l., Via Felice Casati 20, I-20124 Milano*

In France: Please write to *Penguin France S. A., 17 rue Lejeune, F–31000 Toulouse*

In Japan: Please write to *Penguin Books Japan, Ishikiribashi Building, 2–5–4, Suido, Bunkyo-ku, Tokyo 112*

In Greece: Please write to *Penguin Hellas Ltd, Dimocritou 3, GR–106 71 Athens*

In South Africa: Please write to *Longman Penguin Southern Africa (Pty) Ltd, Private Bag X08, Bertsham 2013*